THE AN

Gwenda Bond is a freel
was a regular contribut
travelled to Brazil to view overseas mission for herself, and
has also produced Bible Study material for the Bible Society
in conjunction with the Baptist Union. She is based in
Derby and is married to a Baptist minister.

THE
ANSWERED
CALL

William Carey and
The Dawn of Modern Mission

GWENDA BOND

Marshall Pickering
An Imprint of HarperCollinsPublishers

Marshall Pickering is an imprint of
HarperCollins*Religious*,
Part of HarperCollins*Publishers*,
77–85 Fulham Palace Road, London W6 8JB

First published in Great Britain
in 1992 by Marshall Pickering

1 3 5 7 9 10 8 6 4 2

A catalogue record for this book is
available from the British Library

ISBN 0 551 02711 8

Printed and bound in Great Britain by
HarperCollinsManufacturing Glasgow

Contents

1. Death in a Strange Land

The beginnings of the BMS

The day they buried little Peter, Dorothy Carey thought that her heart would break. It was not, of course, a new experience for her to lose a child. Few women at the end of the eighteenth century were spared that particular pain. Dorothy closed her eyes against the glare of the Indian sun and remembered how they had laid little Ann, just two years old, to rest in the Northamptonshire village that was home. They had buried her in unconsecrated ground, of course, for they were Dissenters. But at least Ann had been lovingly laid where spring sunshine melted the snows, where hawthorn studded the spreading hedgerows and where cobblers sat in their cottages cutting and stitching leather as William once had done.

But this, this was different, this death in an alien and unloving land. Five-year-old Peter had died of dysentery; small wonder when they were eking out a living on an indigo plantation frequently sodden in flood. They had had a hard time of it even to find someone to bury the child's body. Hindus, Dorothy discovered, do not usually bury their dead, committing them instead to fire or water. And which of the local men would agree to lose caste by performing such a task? Eventually they had found four Muslims prepared to dig the grave, and Peter had gone. Staring at the grave the next day, Dorothy gathered her other sons, Felix, William and Jabez, the youngest, fiercely against her, terrified in her loneliness of further loss.

For how could she talk to William, even in her lucid moments, which she knew with sickening dread were becoming less and less frequent? How could she talk to William who, though he had been ill himself, was even now working with his pundit translating Scripture into Bengali?

'Scripture' for Dorothy was something that she had heard read aloud in the tiny chapel in Hackleton, as they had read aloud the hymns, line by line, for a congregation that could neither read nor write. But that had not been enough for William. Never mind that he had had little formal education; William was keenly intelligent and spiritually determined. His innate gift for languages and his belief that the Christian Gospel was for every nationality had come together in a compulsion to translate the Scriptures into the language of Bengal. That compulsion, together with his preaching to the small European community in the area of Dinajpur, filled every moment spared from the work of this indigo plantation.

Dorothy turned from the small grave. The boys, seizing their chance, ran ahead but she moved slowly, oppressed by the heat. India, she knew, was destroying her, as it had destroyed lively little Peter. But how could she talk to William, preoccupied with study and preaching, about this land and this death?

*

If Dorothy Carey was already predisposed towards mental illness, perhaps of the type that we would today describe as 'paranoia', it was hardly surprising that the events of the past few months should have threatened to push her over the edge.

She had been five months pregnant when William had announced that he and John Thomas, a ship's surgeon with experience of life in Bengal – and a colourful experience it later turned out to be – were to go to India as the first missionaries of the Particular Baptist Missionary Society. Would Dorothy go with him?

She was, not surprisingly, shocked and afraid. Dorothy had loved William from the moment they had met in the unpretentious dissenting meeting house in Hackleton where her father was a deacon. She had been proud of his self-taught abilities as linguist and preacher; proud when he had published a book, *An Enquiry into the Obligation of Christians to use Means for the Conversion of the Heathen*. She had been grateful too, for the hours he had spent patiently teaching her to read and write.

She had watched from the shadows, busy with her babies, as he had argued the case for a mission to the heathen overseas, and seen his joy as the idea was finally taken up. She had met his friends, Andrew Fuller, John Ryland, John Sutcliffe, and knew what their support meant to William in the furtherance of this dream. But nothing that had happened had prepared her for this shock. How could she – who had found moving from her Northamptonshire home to the town of Leicester when William became pastor of the Harvey Lane church hard enough – go to India? She had three small boys and another on the way. She had never even seen the sea.

So she had said 'No.' And that day in the indigo plantation, gathering her children to her and staring agonised at the grave of Peter, she wished with all her heart that she had stuck to her 'No.' But the departure of William and John Thomas from England that early summer of 1793 had been delayed. They had had time to rush back from the south coast and plead with her once more to go too. By then baby Jabez – she had chosen a Hebrew name meaning 'born in sorrow' – was in her arms, and Dorothy weakened. She would go if her sister Kitty would go with her.

The voyage to Bengal had taken five months during which time the ship, *The Kron Princessa Maria*, had never put into port. Travel by sea in the 1790s was fraught with danger. Britain was at war spasmodically both with France (and one of Napoleon's grand designs was to starve the trade-dependent British into submission) and with the American colonies. Kind as the captain of the *Kron Princessa* was, the journey for Dorothy and Kitty, caring for the boys and the baby in the cramped confines of a boat alternately battered by storms and tantalizingly becalmed, was an extended nightmare. William was busy learning Bengali from John Thomas. He had not forgotten the taunt of those opposed to his ideas: 'What, sir, can you preach in Arabic or Persic, in Hindustani or Bengali, that you think it our duty to send the Gospel to the heathen?'

And when they finally arrived in Bengal – what then? Then they had had to slip under cover up the Hooghly river like the illegal immigrants they were. Bengal was effectively controlled by the East India Company, part trading company but part political and administrative body backed up by their own troops. The closing years of the eighteenth century were nervous times. The French Revolution and the American struggle for independence had spelled out bloodily what could happen if people were not kept in their place. The East India Company wanted no truck with missionaries. Company chaplains toeing the company line, were tolerable; dissenting 'enthusiasts' who might cause unrest and upset the structure on which wealth and power depended were not. There were no permits for missionaries. No welcome then, for the Careys from this land, but a furtive fearful entry.

And no money and no home. Dorothy was hardly worldly-wise, but even she could see – and knew from the grim expression on William's face that he saw too – that John

Thomas, for all his big-hearted love both of his Lord and of the people of Bengal – was hardly an asset. He was permanently in debt yet continued to try to live as if he were not. Creditors pursued him. The money raised in England intended to support the first missionaries for a year, disappeared in days. William had no work. Dorothy's children, weakened by the month on board ship, had dysentery. Were they now going to starve too? To starve to death in this land which was hot, filthy, noisy, bustling with people speaking dozens of languages that left Dorothy's head spinning, terrifying beyond anything she had ever known?

At last an opportunity for work presented itself to William, who had been clear in his *Enquiry* that missionaries must be self-supporting. He became manager of an indigo plantation in Mudnabati in the province of Dinajpur. Dorothy found that she had exchanged the newly-enclosed fields and hills of Northamptonshire for vast flat lands watered by the Ganges, where the reddish-yellow flowers of the indigo shrub gave no hint of the deep blue that would be released when the plants were soaked and beaten.

It was a lonely post. William supervised a workforce of ninety Indians but there were no other Europeans nearby. By then Dorothy had lost the help and support of her sister Kitty, who had married soon after their arrival in India. The plantation was alternately shrivelled by drought and washed by floods. William spent every moment he could working on his translation of Scripture into Bengali. When he came to tell her how he was progressing with Genesis or Exodus, Matthew or Mark, he would smile and draw her into his arms consolingly. 'There's so much to be done,' he explained. 'It's only the people of the higher castes who speak Bengali anyway. To reach the poorest simplest people with the news of the Saviour I must learn Hindustani and the many other tongues they speak. I'm beginning to see that I must also master Sanskrit. That's the language of their own great books and the mother-tongue of all the others. You do see . . . ?' he begged her.

And Dorothy would ty to see. She would try to smile, for William's faith was her faith too; otherwise she would not have been here at all. But her harsh introduction into India had been too exhausting, physically and emotionally, for her. Peter had been claimed by this strange land. There were days when Felix and William ran unheeded and uncared for through the plantation, little Jabez in their wake, while their mother was imprisoned in a sick and sad and lonely mind.

*

The Particular Baptist Missionary Society, which had sent William Carey and John Thomas to India as its first missionaries, had been formed by a handful of men meeting in a house in Kettering on 2nd October 1792.

Carey has been described as 'the founder of modern missions' and in many ways it would be true to say that what happened that autumn day was the result of his vision and the doggedness with which he had pursued it. But it would also be true to say that it was the result of the coming together of a group of like-minded men who were themselves shaped by the turbulent age in which they found themselves.

The world was changing, internationally, industrially, politically, spiritually. New areas of the globe were opening up. The accounts of Captain Cook's voyages in the 1770s had reached the cottage in Paulerspury, Northamptonshire, where William Carey grew up and had captured his imagination. So had the travels of his uncle in Canada. There was intense rivalry in trade between the Spanish, Portuguese, Dutch, French and British, a commitment and energy also not lost on the young Carey. Look what other men would hazard for the sake of commerce and financial gain; how much more should Christians dare for the sake of the Gospel!

The Industrial Revolution was changing the face of Britain, enlarging its towns and cutting new paths of transport between them. Labour was being organized at best, exploited at worst, and life for those who had worked for themselves in their own cottages, weavers like William's father, shoemakers like William himself, would never be the same again.

Great social unrest and uprisings in France and in America had argued for the inalienable rights of the individual. New notions of democracy pushed at old bastions of aristocracy and autocracy. In England, Christians like William Wilberforce and his friends in what was known as the 'Clapham sect' shared that vision, that longing for men and women to be free. But they saw too that people had not only rights but needs – the need to be forgiven, to find peace and joy, the need to hear the Gospel of Jesus Christ. The religious formality of the eighteenth century, 'the age of reason', was shown for the empty sham it was by the Evangelical Revival, which set personal faith in Christ before all else.

Remarkable times produce remarkable people. In the small Baptist world of the East Midlands, some remarkable men came together. Andrew Fuller, pastor of the church at Kettering, was a man whose mind was as energetic as his body was big and his heart was warm. Though like his friends a Particular Baptist, he had moved away from the hyper-Calvinism of his upbringing, that saw no need for evangelism since only God's 'elect' were to be saved, to the belief that the good news of salvation through faith in Christ was for everyone. In writing *The Gospel Worthy of All Acceptation*, he had stirred up a theological debate about predestination.

Then there was the scholarly and sensitive John Ryland

who shared his father's pastorate at College Lane, North-ampton, but was soon to be Principal of the Baptist Academy in Bristol and pastor of the Broadmead Church. He was discovering all he could about events in America: the work of Jonathan Edwards, missionary to the Red Indians, and the 'great awakening' of religious faith in Massachussets.

His friend, Yorkshireman John Sutcliffe, was Baptist pastor at Olney, where the former slave-trader John Newton was Anglican curate. Sutcliffe, though ever cautious, shared Ryland's conviction about the significance of events in America, and had called on Baptists in Northamptonshire to pray for revival in their own area.

Into the lives of these men, who had the intelligence, the wisdom and the spirituality to respond to the signs of the times, had come Carey; Carey the cobbler-cum-schoolmaster-cum preacher and pastor; Carey whose weaver father had himself become a schoolmaster; Carey who, with limited access to books, had taught himself Greek, Hebrew, Latin, French, Italian and Dutch; Carey who had set down on paper his conviction that it was time for a mission to the heathen overseas.

In a concise book of eighty-seven pages, *An Enquiry into the Obligation of Christians to use Means for the Conversion of the Heathen Overseas*, Carey had set out all the information he had gleaned about the geography, population and religion of lands he could barely dream of. He charted them carefully in continents.

ASIA

Countries	Length Miles	Breadth Miles	Number of Inhabitants	Religion
Isle of Ceylon	250	200	2,000,000	Pagans, except Dutch Church
Maldives	1000 in number		100,000	Mahametans
Sumatra	1000	100	2,100,000	Ditto and Pagans
Java	580	100	2,700,000	Ditto
Timor	240	54	300,000	Ditto and a few Christians

His *Survey of the Present State of the World* and its charts filled twenty-eight pages.

In that short work, too, Carey had expounded his belief that, if the early church could engage in missionary activity and so more recently could the Jesuits and the Moravians, then so could the dissenting church of his day.

Into that pamphlet Carey had poured his conviction that Jesus' command to go into all the world and preach the Gospel was binding not on the first apostles alone but on all his followers. If these ideas do not sound new to us now, they came as a timebomb at the end of the urbane, rational, orderly eighteenth century. To be 'enthusiastic' or 'over the top' as we might put it today was frowned on. Carey had been rebuked for enthusiasm by his elders: 'Sit down, young man. When God chooses to convert the heathen, he will do it without your aid or mine.'

Such an attitude did not stop Carey writing his book, especially since he had found sympathetic hearts in Fuller, Ryland and Sutcliffe and in Samuel Pearce, a Birmingham Baptist willing to finance its printing. Neither did it stop him preaching at the Whitsuntide Assembly of the Baptist Association at Nottingham on 30th May 1792. For Carey the words from Isaiah 54:2–3, 'Enlarge the place of thy tent', could mean only one thing: 'Move on. Move out.' It was in this sermon that he preached the immortal line, 'Expect great things from God. Attempt great things for God.'

It was and would come to be known as 'a deathless sermon'.

So eventually fourteen men had come together in the home of Mrs Martha Wallis in Kettering on 2nd October 1792. 'Gospel Inn' that home was nicknamed because of the warmth of welcome and strength of faith found there, a warmth and strength undiminished by the recent death of Martha's husband, a deacon in Fuller's church.

The ministers had heard John Ryland preach that morning on Isaiah 43:13, 'I shall work and who shall let it?' Nothing was going to 'let' or hinder them now. For a small group of young dissenting ministers to form a missionary society was an incredible undertaking. The £13.12.6 pledged in subscriptions that day and placed in a snuff box represented in each case around one week's wages. But it represented too a promise on the part of each man to play his part in enabling the good news of Jesus Christ who had transformed their lives to transform also the lives of people whom they would never meet.

Each of the men there was to play his part in 'The Particular Baptist Society for the Propagation of the Gospel amongst the Heathen' in a different way. Ryland, as Principal in Bristol, was to encourage his students into service overseas. Sutcliffe, having established a smaller academy at Olney, was to train many of the early missionary candidates. Fuller was the first Secretary of the Society and was to travel the length and breadth of the country raising money and enthusiasm for its work. He was to see other missionary societies – the London Missionary Society (LMS), the Church Missionary Society (CMS), the British and Foreign Bible Society and American missions – coming to birth. But Carey himself, it soon transpired, was to go to India. Ahead of him lay the struggling years in Mudnabati but then the community at Serampore.

*

Colonel Bie, Governor of the Danish settlement of Serampore, found himself in a quandary. The arrival of travellers in the town was hardly a rare occurrence, for Serampore, strategically placed on the west bank of the Hooghly river, about fifteen miles north of Calcutta, was nothing if not cosmopolitan. The ships that plied the wide stretch of water sailed under almost every flag. Across on the other bank, regiments of East India Company troops were stationed at Barrackpore. From the window where he stood pondering what to do about the new arrivals, he saw a main street thronging not only with Indians, mainly Hindus, but with the features of almost every European country – not only Danes but French, German, Dutch, English and Portuguese.

Colonel Bie wanted good relations with the British. But this latest group of strangers to arrive in Serampore, odder and wearier than most, bore a letter of commendation from the Danish embassy. Clearly, someone of influence somewhere was on their side. Colonel Bie himself was a Christian and it was a somewhat bedraggled group of Christians, who stood hopefully before him now. It was October 1799 and a new contingent of Baptist missionaries, having sailed on an American ship, *The Criterion*, had arrived in India.

Colonel Bie's eyes travelled from face to face. The Brunsdens, William Ward, young Mary Tidd who had come to marry John Fountain, already with Carey. He smiled at the small children of the Grants and the Marshmans and Hannah Marshman caught his eye. She was not the kind of woman to be afraid, but she knew that she needed help for her family and her new friends.

Because the indigo plantation in Mudnabati had finally closed, deluged out of existence, Carey had planned for the new missionaries to go to him on another plantation in Kidderpore in North Bengal. As far as the East India

Company was concerned, however, missionaries were still a development to be resisted. 'You have no permits,' Colonel Bie explained gently. 'The East India Company will send you back the minute they have the opportunity. I think you will find that to go to Kidderpore is out of the question. You may, however . . .' He paused and looked again at the faces of the children, pale from months at sea. 'You may settle here, if you wish. There has been a Moravian mission, you know, in Serampore until very recently. They found it hard. The influence of the Brahmans is very strong. But, who knows, you may have more success. Yes, you may settle here and you may ask your brother Carey to join you.'

Over the next few months the interest and care for the Baptist missionaries shown by Colonel Bie that day was to grow. He watched their tragedies. William Grant died of fever within three weeks. Mary Tidd was pregnant when widowed within a year. Carey arrived in Serampore with a wife now so sick that Hannah Marshman, busy already with the bereaved Mrs Grant and her children, had known at once that she had three more boys to care for – and unruly ones used to doing as they pleased.

For all that, it was clear to Colonel Bie that the missionaries intended to stay. They purchased a large house in two acres of ground on the river bank. Here the missionary families were to live as a community, ordered in many ways as the Moravians had ordered theirs. They were discovering each other's friendship and each other's gifts – and it was clear that they needed room.

William Ward was just what Carey had hoped and prayed for – a printer. Carey had set up a small press of his own in Mudnabati but now with Ward's expertise and helped by Brunsden, the printing of the Bengali New Testament could really get under way.

Joshua Marshman was a teacher and he and Hannah had plans for a much-needed school for the children of

Europeans. Yes, the house had to be large, a home for all the members of the mission, with space for printing, for a school and for a chapel. It must have gardens, for Carey, a botanist as well as a linguist at heart, loved growing things.

It seemed to Colonel Bie, watching from a distance and then becoming a regular visitor to the mission house, that a home for ten adults and nine children was to take some running and some financing.

'One man of the wrong temper,' William Ward observed, 'could make our home a hell.'

Ward himself was a gentle and patient personality. If Hannah Marshman took over the rôle of mother to Dorothy's sons, William Ward developed a fatherly relationship with them and helped each of them to find a personal Christian faith. Nevertheless, tensions were inevitable and had to be quickly defused. On Saturday evenings all the members of the community gathered to discuss the week's work and to pray. This was a much-needed opportunity to vent feelings, to right relationships, and to ensure that decisions were taken jointly.

A shortage of money in the early days must have added to the tensions. In 1800, however, Joshua and Hannah were able to open their planned boarding schools for European and Anglo-Indian boys and girls. Profits from these schools, in the region of £1000, were to become the financial mainstay of the mission.

The more Colonel Bie saw of Hannah Marshman, the more his first instincts about her were confirmed. He visited the mission house one evening as the missionaries' children, together with the boarders from the school, played in the grounds. Their laughter vied with the clatter of the printing presses. Hannah was up to her eyes in work in the kitchen, checking not only the stores of food but a consignment of medicines recently arrived from England. The struggle against the climate and disease did not let up, but neither did it seem to sap Hannah's energy and warmth. There was, she explained to Colonel Bie, more to be done.

'The boarding schools for European children are important to us,' she explained. 'Almost every day we get new enquiries from parents delighted to find that we can teach geometry, Latin, Greek, grammar . . . But other children need education too. So we are setting up a free school for Bengali boys.'

Within six weeks, Colonel Bie observed, that school had over forty pupils. It was not to be long before one hundred schools, teaching 10,000 pupils with Indian teachers, were established around Serampore.

*

The strands of the mission's work were coming together. As Hannah knew, people had to be literate in order to read for themselves the Word of God. Baptists, stressing the authority and centrality in worship of the Word, had no doubt that Scripture could speak for itself. But people also needed Scripture in their own language. Eight and later ten printing presses clattered away in Serampore and on 5th March 1801 the first complete New Testament in Bengali was bound and laid on the Communion table in the chapel that was the heart of the community in the house by the river.

The missionaries, however, had come not only to translate but also to proclaim a liberating message to people on whom the Hindu caste system laid rigid constraints. In that area progress was far more elusive. During the years in Dinajpur, Carey had preached to the small European community and established a small Baptist church. He had tried patiently to point the Hindus who worked for him to a God who cared for all his creatures individually and equally; a God who offered immediate access to himself through

Jesus; a God whose love and forgiveness did not have to be earned but was freely offered. He had preached in the villages to crowds of Hindus, questioning them about their own faith, always with deference, for he knew that 'to insult a man's religion is not the mode best calculated to win his confidence'. His hearers listened politely but none of those who heard him made any response.

That lack of response threatened to sap Carey's energy and destroy his hope. It threatened to stifle even that sense of 'expectancy' that had been the keynote of his formative address in Nottingham. He could not share his discouragement with Dorothy, whom he referred to in his letters to Andrew Fuller now as 'my domestic affliction'. But to his friends in England he could on paper at least pour out his heart.

'I am grown almost callous,' he had written to Pearce in 1799, 'and am tempted to preach as if their hearts were invulnerable.'

How long would he have to wait for one Indian to grasp and profess what it meant to be a follower of Jesus? And how long before he could act against some of the cruelties that were part of the Hindu culture? Carey's first experience of *sati* had burned deeply into his consciousness. It was hard to describe the horror of that, too, to Andrew Fuller 15,000 miles away in a very different culture, but he had to try. Those who were, as they put it, 'holding the ropes' at home needed to glimpse some of the depths of the mine into which the overseas missionaries had clambered down.

'As I was returning fom Calcutta,' he wrote, his mind still seething, 'I saw the Sahamaranam, or, a woman burning herself with the corpse of her husband, for the first time in my life . . . Before evening we got out of the boat to walk when we saw a number of people assembled on the riverside. I asked them what they were met for, and they told me to burn the body of a dead man. I inquired if his wife would

die with him; they answered Yes, and pointed to the woman
. . . I began to exclaim with all my might about what they
were doing, telling them it was a shocking murder. They
told me it was a great act of holiness . . .

'I exhorted the woman not to throw away her life; to fear
nothing, for no evil would follow her refusal to burn. But
she in the most calm manner mounted the pile, and danced
on it with her hands extended, as if in the utmost tranquillity
of spirit . . . . Then she lay down by the corpse, and put one
arm under its neck and the other over it, when a quantity of
dry cocoa-leaves and other substances were heaped over
them to a considerable height, and then ghee, or melted
preserved butter, poured on the top. Two bamboos were
then put over them and held fast down, and fire put to the
pile . . .

'No sooner was the fire kindled than all the people set up a
great shout – Hurree Bol, Hurree Bol, which is a common
shout of joy, and an invocation of Hurree or Seeb. It was
impossible to have heard the women had she groaned or
even cried aloud, on account of the mad noise of the people,
and it was impossible for her to stir or struggle on account of
the bamboos which were held down on her like the levers of
a press.'

Carey witnessed many ritual burnings, often of girls only
in their early teens, often of women who tried in vain to
struggle from the flames. His horror at it never diminished
and he begged successive Governors General to forbid it,
but he had to wait until December 1830, thirty-six years
after his arrival in India, for *sati* to be made illegal.

Despite the discouragement the missionaries often felt
when preaching, they did not have to wait thirty-six years
for their first Indian convert. In October 1800 the volatile
John Thomas, who had spent many years doing who-
knew-what with no contact with Carey, appeared at
Serampore. He found the children who had sailed with him

on the *Kron Princessa* growing up and fifteen-year-old Felix preaching to the local people alongside Ward. Perhaps the busy but settled and loving community at Serampore was just what John Thomas needed, after all his wanderings. He stayed on and so was at hand when one November morning a Bengali carpenter, Krishna Pal, slipped and dislocated his shoulder on the steps leading down into the Ganges.

John Thomas, called to help, had the opportunity to chat to Krishna Pal in his own language.

'A carpenter, are you?' he asked, manipulating the shoulder. 'Have you heard of a carpenter called Jesus?'

Krishan Pal had not. What he did have, however, was a sense of sin, a sense of his own failings and need, to which Hinduism did not speak.

'I can give you something to take away the pain,' Thomas promised as he set the shoulder. 'But only Jesus can take away sin.'

Just one month later Colonel Bie was one of a group of Europeans and Indians, including Krishna Pal's wife, her sister and her daughter (who were later to become Christians themselves), gathered on the bank of the Ganges, the river holy to Hindus. They had come to witness the Christian baptism of Krishna and of Felix Carey.

Colonel Bie recalled that day the tired group of parents and children who had arrived on his doorstep with no permit to be in India. He recalled his warning to them of how sadly fruitless the Moravian effort had been. Now he listened as Ward preached in English and Carey in Bengali and joined in the Bengali hymn. He watched as Carey led Krishna Pal and Felix into the water for believers' baptism.

He was not the only Dane to share that moment. Near him was Charlotte Rumohr, a wealthy and educated but disabled woman. Charlotte had come to live near the mission house and had observed there something that had been lacking in her Lutheran upbringing. She sensed that day that it could not be long before she herself must profess her growing Christian faith in baptism.

*

It was the day they had looked for and prayed for. But, as the baptisms took place, two lonely and sick people were in the cool shadows of the mission house. John Thomas, having been instrumental in the conversion of Krishna, had subsequently fallen into a state of mental illness from which he never recovered. And there was Dorothy. She must have sensed that Hannah Marshman, out there on the river bank sharing in the celebration, had become more of a mother to her son than she herself had been able to be. Perhaps that hurt her. And perhaps it was as well that her confused mind could not grasp that Charlotte Rumohr was to be the second Mrs Carey and was to become, with her intellectual ability and gift for languages, a soul-mate for Carey.

Yet for those who shared it, it was a great and significant day. Krishna Pal was to become the first native missionary to Calcutta and then to Assam.

'The chain of the caste is broken,' rejoiced William Ward. 'Who shall mend it?'

In fact conversions would always be slow and painfully achieved in India. By the time Carey had been in India twenty years, there were about 600 Christians and a few thousand supporters, many of them enduring physical and mental persecution, rejected by family and community. Apart from localized 'explosions' of Christian faith in the Kond Hills and Mizoram in later years, the work of making new Christians in India was to remain painstaking and difficult. But that November day the chain of the caste *was* broken, and a tiny harvest was reaped from seeds that had been sown, often with heavy hearts. Here was news for the faithful friends in England.

'We have toiled so long and have met with so many discouragements,' wrote Carey, 'but at last the Lord has appeared for us.'

2. Uphill Work

India to 1840

The baptism of Krishna Pal was followed by that of his sister-in-law, his wife and his friend, Gokul. Before long a Brahman and a kayust, a member of the writer caste, came to the point where they were prepared to lose caste in sharing in the Lord's Supper. As Hindus became Christians, the missionaries had repeatedly to make it clear that there was no place for any vestige of caste within the Christian fellowship, in which all were one in Christ Jesus. The one-time high-caste Brahman was to receive Communion after the one-time low-caste sudra.

There were other battles to be fought, political in nature yet no less spiritual for that. At stake still was the freedom, indeed the right, to proclaim the Gospel in India. The missionary families remained in India under sufferance, protected at Serampore by the Danish flag, though the small colony was to change hands between Britain and Denmark several times in the next few decades. But they were not content for their work to be confined to Serampore. Now that there were Indian Christians whom they could train, they were eager to set up a chain of mission stations inland where native evangelists could play their part. They had plans for a chapel in Calcutta. Yet their status remained uncertain and dependent on the goodwill of the Governor General.

For a while they enjoyed such goodwill. Governor General Wellesley was a far-seeing man, courageous enough to stand up to the pressure groups within the East

India Company. He was troubled to see young men, sometimes only fifteen years old, sent from England to work in the Indian Civil Service with no knowledge of the language and culture of the area they were to administer. When he decided to set up the Fort William College in Calcutta to train them, it was to Carey that he turned to be 'tutor' – because as a Dissenter Carey would not sign the 39 articles of faith of the Church of England, he could not for some years be designated 'professor' – in Bengali.

How could the Hackleton cobbler, acutely aware of his own lack of formal education, stand before the young products of the English public school system? In desperation he wrote to his more academic friend John Ryland: 'I am almost sunk under the prospect, having never known college exercises is a great weight on my mind. Give me your counsel and your prayers.'

Yet, though it took all Carey's courage and faith to accept it, the Fort William appointment was important. In appointing him, Wellesley was clearly demonstrating to the anti-missionary faction in India the personal respect he had for Carey. His new rôle gave Carey an opportunity to influence young men who were to be instrumental in the government of India; of Carey's first forty-five students, twenty-one went on to become judges. Throughout the world for the next 200 years missionaries were to play a vital role in educating men who would have a formative part to play in the government of their country. William's son, Jabez, brought to Christian faith J. W. Ricketts, who brought about the abolition of the colour-bar from the Indian Civil Service.

Carey's appointment brought with it a salary of 500 rupees a month, a welcome addition to the income from Hannah and Joshua Marshman's schools in financing the growing work of the mission and the costly translations. He ws already revising his Bengali New Testament. The longer he stayed in India, the more he recognized that much of his early work was 'English' in idiom and style. Meanwhile Joshua was beginning a study of Chinese that was to culminate in his translation of the Bible into Chinese in 1823. Preparing type and printing was very expensive. As Carey took his place in the lecture rooms of Calcutta, 15,000 miles away Andrew Fuller was travelling the hills and valleys of Northern England and Scotland, from scattered congregation to congregation, raising money for the translation of the Scriptures in India. He journeyed 1,300 miles and raised £1 for every mile he travelled.

The sympathy and support of Wellesley cheered the small community at Serampore. The first nonconformist chapel in Calcutta was opened in the Lall Bazar. The news from home was that the society had appointed new missionaries for the work in India. But storm clouds were gathering. The political climate changed dramatically when Wellesley was recalled. Lord Cornwallis arrived in India, already exhausted by years of colonial service, and died within two months. The anti-missionary party seized their opportunity to lobby the stand-in Governor, Sir George Barlow. Attempts to convert Hindus to Christianity, they insisted, were destabilizing to the company, the government, indeed the Empire. Very soon two events occurred which they were able to construe as evidence of their argument.

The first was a mutiny of Indian soldiers at Vellore. Vellore was a volatile area with anti-government agitation caused by adherents of a former sultan. A British army officer was more than foolhardy, therefore, when he attempted to introduce a rule that the soldiers should dispense with any distinguishing marks of caste, should shave and should wear a new style turban more akin to a hat. The sepoys mutinied, killing over a hundred British soldiers, and the mutiny was suppressed with the death of four hundred Indians.

The panic that ensued in India and in London rebounded on the missionaries. 'Look what happened,' their adversaries cried, 'when any attempt was made to interfere with the religious customs of the Hindu.' Hard on the heels of the Vellore mutiny rose another cause of dissension. An over-zealous Muslim convert, entrusted with translating a tract at Serampore, took the opportunity to add some sentences of his own pouring scorn on Mohammed. The Serampore missionaries recognized they were at fault in not checking the work but they were not prepared for the full weight of the new Governor General, Lord Minto, to descend on them. Their tracts were to be submitted to him for approval. There was to be no extension of the work beyond Serampore, no preaching in Lall Bazar. John Chater and William Robinson, who had made an untimely arrival on the *Benjamin Franklin*, were not to be allowed to settle in Bengal. It seemed as if every door was closing and the home they had made in Serampore suddenly appeared more akin to a prison. 'We are all of us in prison in Serampore,' Carey grieved, but he drew comfort from Scriptural precedents. 'We are in much the same position as the Apostles when commanded not to preach any more in the Name.'

In fact, as so often happens, as one door closed, the Lord opened another. Robinson, denied access to Bengal, went instead to the desolate area of Bhutan and later to Java, where he used copies of Marshman's Chinese translation of the gospels amongst the Chinese population there. Chater went to Burma, where he was joined in Rangoon by Felix Carey. Five years later he went to Colombo in Ceylon, where he worked for seventeen years, translating the Scriptures into Singhalese.

Gradually the relationship between the Baptist mission-aries and Lord Minto eased. But for how long could their status and the progress of the mission be dependent on the attitude of the Governor General and on circumstances such as Vellore? It was time for a decisive battle over the right to proclaim the Gospel. That was a battle that could not be engaged in India alone.

*

Andrew Fuller sat alone in his study in Kettering. It was growing dark but, from his window, under a scudding sky, he could just see the church where tomorrow his people would gather for worship. He was still their beloved pastor, caring for them through dark years of war with both Napoleon and America. The British economy was being strangled and often his people queued in the market-place for limited supplies of food that were almost beyond their means. At times he agonized over the fact that, when his people needed so much spiritual encouragement, at least a quarter of his time these days was spent, not in the pulpit at Kettering or in the homes of his congregation, but in the work of the Missionary Society. The more gladly his people relinquished him, the more dearly he loved them for it.

But tonight, early in 1813, he was weary, mentally, physically, spiritually, as he tried to summon his strength for the one last struggle to come. He was weary of mental effort and argument. On his desk lay a copy of his pamphlet *An Apology for Christian Mission*. In it he had put the case for toleration in India – but toleration not only for the religions of the Hindu and of the Muslim but toleration too for the work of Christian mission.

He was weary also of physical exertion and of travelling. He still recalled as if with a physical blow the news he had received on 18th September 1812, of fire at Serampore the previous March. By then the whole Bible had been translated into Bengali, the New Testament into Sanskrit, the New Testament and Psalms into Oriya, the Gospels into

Hindustani. Pundits in every language worked alongside native workmen cutting characters for the type. Then in one night fire had razed the printing house. Reams of paper, valuable manuscripts, copies of Scripture, all were lost, though in the ashes next morning the stunned missionaries had found the precious mounts for the type that took so long to cut.

Fuller's big heart had ached for his friends, though he knew their resilience and determination and had not been surprised by Carey's reaction. 'Much ground must be laboured over again and I have suffered most. But we are not discouraged. We are chastened but not killed, cast down but not destroyed, perplexed but not in despair.'

Andrew Fuller had longed at that moment to be with the friends he had not seen for fourteen years, to weep with those who wept. Instead he had poured his energy into raising in weeks the money needed to replace the work of years. His people in England virtually had no bread to eat; yet to his door his own church members brought £160. Baptists in Edinburgh sent £800; the Bristol churches £400; Moulton chapel £50. The story touched the hearts not of Baptists alone but of all the Free Churches and many Anglican congregations. The loss in Serampore had been estimated at between £9,000 and £10,000. It was made good in two months. In the process the work there received a publicity it had never had before.

But Fuller's years of exhortation and of travel had taken their toll and he knew tonight what still lay ahead of him if he were faithfully to 'hold the ropes' for his friends. The East India Company's Charter was due for revision. Prime Minister Castlereagh had made it clear that he saw no reason for significant change in it, certainly not for the granting of licences to missionaries. Some members of the company had adopted the stance of positively extolling the virtues of Hinduism, so that Charles Grant, a Director and a

Christian, had been led to observe bitterly in England that 'Almost all men of influence appeared to act on the conviction that duty and success lay in stifling Christianity, whilst they manifested the most delicate regard to the wildest super-stitions of the heathen.' In India Carey lamented: 'I mourn on my country's account that preaching the Gospel should be regarded in the same light as committing a felony.'

Castlereagh had to be brought to change his mind. The people in the churches in England had to be roused to bring pressure to bear, pressure that would counteract the influential voices in India House. The struggle to legalize the position of Christian missions could not be postponed. But had Fuller the strength for it?

At least he was not alone. From the pile of papers on his desk Andrew pulled the article that Robert Southey had written a few years previously in the *Quarterly Review*, and his heart was warmed by the words before his tired eyes. 'Only fourteen years have elapsed since Thomas and Carey set foot in India, and in that time these missionaries have acquired this gift of tongues. In fourteen years these low-born, low-bred mechanics have done more to spread the knowledge of the Scriptures among the heathen than has been accomplished or even attempted by all the world beside.'

Fuller knew that other missionary societies – the Church Missionary Society, the London Missionary Society and the Methodists – were also ready to battle over Castlereagh's India Bill. And he knew that, while he, Fuller, rallied the Baptists, William Wilberforce, who counted the cause of Christian missions as dear as the abolition of the slave trade, would rally the Church of England.

It was now quite dark as Fuller prayed alone in his study. But he was not alone. He knew that the Lord would supply the strength he needed.

★

The resolution put to the Commons by a reluctant Prime Minister ran thus: 'That it is the duty of this country to promote the interest and happiness of the inhabitants of the British Dominion in India, and that such means ought to be adopted as may lead to the introduction among them of useful knowledge and of religious and moral improvement. That in the furtherance of the above objects sufficient facilities should be afforded by law to persons desirous of going to and remaining in India for the purpose of accomplishing these benevolent designs.'

For months Castlereagh had been deluged under what Fuller described as not so much a 'shower' as a 'set rain' of 900 petitions in favour of Christian missions. Now, as debate raged in both Houses, Wellesley gave personal testimony in the Lords to the work of the missionaries in India and the ageing but still passionate Wilberforce used all his eloquence for three hours in the Commons.

Even as the resolution was being won, Castlereagh attempted to play down its significance.

'I do not consider,' he said, 'that there is any ground for supposing that any dread will be created in the minds of the Hindus. The voyage to India is long and the expense of it great; I am inclined to believe that the spirit of proselytism is not so exuberant in our times as to tempt any very alarming number of persons to proceed on religious missions to India.'

He could not have been more wrong in his predictions. Within months of the bill becoming law, Andrew Fuller had obtained a licence from India House for Carey's nephew Eustace to go to India. Over the next few years Eustace was to be followed by Yates, from the Harvey Lane Church, Leicester, where William himself had been minister, by schoolteacher Penney and by Samuel Pearce's son, a printer. All now seemed set fair for the work in Bengal to expand, but there was bitterness and sorrow to come.

Into the campaign for the revision of the Charter in the
India Bill, Andrew Fuller had poured the last surge of a
powerful tide of energy. He died exhausted in 1815, one
year after Sutcliffe, and in him the three senior missionaries
in Serampore lost their oldest and dearest friend and ally.
After a two-year period in which John Ryland was
Associate Secretary with James Hinton of Oxford, John
Dyer left the pastorate at Reading to become the new
Secretary. He was a cautious methodical man of integrity
but he had no personal relationship with Carey, Marshman
and Ward to warm his correspondence with them. Carey
was taken aback by the formality of the new relationship.

'All his communications are like those of a Secretary of
State,' he grieved, letter in hand in Serampore. 'Not as
formerly the case with dear brother Fuller, those of a
Christian friend.'

The 'coming of age' of missionary enterprise afforded by
its recognition in the India Bill, twenty-one years after the
humble meeting in the home of Widow Wallis, inevitably
brought with it the new constraints of maturity. Marshman's son was able later to reflect on the significance of the
changes taking place:

'Missions had attained the maturity and organization of a
national enterprise. Missionaries no longer went to India
with the understanding that they must depend for the means
of subsistence mainly on their own exertions . . . The
Societies were enabled to give adequate salaries to their
missionaries and this brought in its train a new principle of
subordination.'

The more formal nature of the administration of the
Society was embodied in a committee enlarged to thirty-
five and in a move of headquarters to London – first to
Wood Street, then to Wardrobe Place and then to Fen
Court, Fenchurch Street. A finance committee was estab-
lished and its priorities were not always those of the

missionaries on the field, whose pulses were quickened by
the opportunities they saw for expansion. As the probably
inevitable trend towards a more directive executive continued, it was decided that the work at Serampore should be
controlled by a group of eleven trustees, made up of the three
senior missionaries there but also of eight trustees in England.

The news that reached Carey, Marshman and Ward in
1817 came as a personal blow against their independence of
spirit and against their integrity. Contrary to rumours
circulating in England that they were amassing personal
fortunes, the three families had poured between £30,000 and
£40,000 of their own earnings into the Serampore site, the
printing house, the schools, the growing chain of mission
stations. They were now preparing to allocate £15,000 of
their own money for the building of a College at
Serampore. Were they to hand over effective control of
their work to trustees whom they had never met? While
Marshman wrote an angry letter on behalf of the three men to
the home committee, Carey turned deeply hurt to Ryland,
his surviving friend who now seemed allied with the new
executive. 'We are yours to live and die with you, but as your
brothers, not your servants. I beseech you, therefore, not to
attempt to exercise a power over us, to which we shall never
submit.'

So began a rift between London and Serampore that,
despite visits home by William Ward, by Hannah Marshman
and finally by her husband, was to last for twenty sad and
bitter years. It was a rift in which the new generation of
looked-for young missionaries was to play its part.

*

Joshua Marshman stormed into the printing house in search
of William Ward. He was in the blackest mood of anger his
colleague had ever known.

'How can they do it?' he thundered above the harsh rattle of the presses. 'How can they do it, not just to us – never mind us! – but to the work of the Lord?'

William became aware that pundits and typesetters had paused in their work and were looking questioningly towards Joshua. Gently William took his arm.

'Walk with me by the river,' he suggested, easing Joshua away from the curious eyes. 'I need a rest and some cooler air myself. Let's talk by the river.'

William knew to which part of the Hooghly bank he was steering his friend but Joshua continued to vent his anger as if heedless of the direction of their steps.

'It's bad enough to deal with that bunch of counting-house men in London,' he raged. 'That's what Ryland called them, did you hear? "I tremble for the ark of God when it shall fall into the hands of mere counting-house men." That's what he said.'

'So do we all,' said Ward gently.

'And daring to suggest that eight men who've never set eyes on the work here should control what we do! That is bad enough. But this!' His voice shook. 'We had such high hopes for these young men. We need their energy and their gifts. The Lord could use them in so many new areas. But they have turned against us, betrayed us.'

'Joshua, they are young and inexperienced,' Ward interposed softly. 'They came out here with fresh ideas, many of them the ideas of this new committee with whom we have such differences. Perhaps it is hard for them to settle into our community here. We've been here so long and are set in our ways.'

'No, it's me,' Joshua said bitterly. 'It's me they can't get along with. You know that. Eustace said the other day that he had no quarrel with his uncle. It's me they dislike and oppose, and it's me they carry tales about to Dyer and his friends.'

Ward was searching for words. He knew in his heart that it was probably true that Eustace Carey, Yates, Pearce, Penney and Lawson had seen in Joshua only the obduracy that could make him a difficult enemy, and not the tenacity and loyalty that made him such a faithful friend.

'But this!' Joshua could hardly bring himself to name what the younger men had done. 'To break away. To set up a rival mission in Calcutta – on our very doorstep, when there are thousands of miles of this benighted land in which the heathen need the good news. They're starting schools, did you know that? They've got a congregation. They have everything they need for a press!'

Ward did know and the actions of the young missionaries grieved him, though with his gentler spirit he could see more of the complexities and difficulties that had arisen than Joshua was prepared to concede at the moment. His colleague was as close to despair as he had ever seen him. But William was directing Joshua's feet to the river bank to revive his hope. Suddenly Marshman realized where they were, on the eighty acres of land they had purchased. At their feet lay the foundations of Serampore College.

William led his friend round the site, pausing now and then to touch the embryonic walls, warm in the Indian sun.

'This will be the museum, Joshua,' he reminded him, 'and this the library. Have you seen the latest plans for the great hall with its two brass staircases? William was talking yesterday about the Ionic pillars there will be at the front – clean classical lines, Joshua, for our college of Eastern Literature and European Science. Think, my friend,' he urged, 'think what we're going to do here.'

'With our £15,000,' Joshua muttered grudgingly. 'The counting-house men shall never get their hands on that.'

'Yes, with our money,' Ward conceded, 'but with help from so many friends too – Lord Hastings, the King of Denmark . . . But *think*,' he repeated, '*hope*, Joshua. Some of

the poorest sons of India as well as some of the richest shall
come here. Caste and creed will be no hindrance. We can
teach them Sanskrit and open up to them the wealth of their
own classics and we can open up to them the newest
advances of Western science. I'm going to England soon
and I shall be looking for a scholar and a Christian to be
professor here. Think, Joshua. You yourself have said that
the Gospel will be spread in India only by the native
evangelist speaking to his Indian brothers whose faith and
culture he knows for himself. Think what an enlightened
education we can offer here, knowing that education cannot
fail to serve the cause of the Gospel. Never mind Eustace
and his Calcutta Missionary Union – time will heal that rift,
my friend. But this, here, this is our way forward now.'

Ward turned his face to Marshman and knew that his
words had struck home.

'William, my dear friend,' said Joshua simply, 'thank
you.' Lost in thought, they turned their steps back to the
printing house.

*

When William Ward returned from a visit to England on
board the *Abberton* in May 1821, he did indeed bring back
with him a professor for the College at Serampore, but a
man who was as much missionary as professor. John Mack,
son of an Edinburgh solicitor, had a very different
background and education from the cobbler, teacher and
printer who had gone to Serampore. He was academically
well qualified for the work ahead of him, with a classical
education but also an interest in science that soon had him
giving chemistry lectures in Serampore. But, having left the
Church of Scotland in order to be baptized as a believer, he
was also of an evangelical and missionary spirit that was to
endear him to the community at Serampore.

There were others on the *Abberton* that day embarking on a new life. There were two strands to the Baptist denomination: the Particular, Calvinistic Baptists who had established the 1792 Society, but also General Baptists who did not subscribe to the doctrine of predestination. Under the influence of tough, lively miner-turned-preacher Dan Taylor, a number of them had formed the 'New Connexion of General Baptists', and they in turn in 1816 had been urged to missionary enterprise.

When John Gregory Pike, minister in Derby, who had pleaded the cause of mission, came aboard to say goodbye to two General Baptist missionaries and their wives, it was for him the fulfilment of a vision.

Pike could not have handed William Bampton, of Great Yarmouth, and James Peggs, who had just left college at Wisbech, into better hands as travelling companions than the experienced William Ward and Hannah Marshman. Ward was to spend the voyage teaching them Bengali, as Thomas had taught Carey – a far cry from the language schools of today. Pike knew too that a loving welcome would await them in Serampore. He urged his friends: 'Cherish a particular regard for that other part of the Baptist denomination who have long been so honourably engaged in the missionary field. The friendship and counsel of such men as their senior missionaries cannot but be a great blessing and comfort to you.'

So started a relationship that was to culminate in the amalgamation of the two societies in 1892. On arrival in India Bampton and Peggs spent three months at Serampore, discussing the area where they should start their work. Finally they felt that the Lord was leading them to Orissa, an area on the eastern coast, south of Calcutta, partly swamp and jungle, prone to flood, partly hilly interior, but also including a cultivated area round Cuttack, where there were around 40,000 inhabitants.

There was in Orissa a great challenge for the missionaries, for at Puri was the site of the temple housing the idol 'Juggernaut', 'Lord of the World'. To this most celebrated Hindu idol came pilgrims from the length and breadth of India, for to die within the precincts of the huge temple and its surroundings was considered to be the passport to eternal bliss. In fact it was the site of cruelty, extortion and violent death of a kind the new missionaries could hardly imagine when they described the area round Puri as 'Satan's headquarters'.

The early years of mission in Orissa were to prove hard indeed. The Bamptons and Peggs were soon joined by the Laceys and the Suttons, but Charlotte Sutton, like Dorothy Carey, lost her reason and died within three months of arriving in India. Both the Bamptons and the Peggs lost children before they had had time to adjust to the new culture, observing 'This adds poignancy to the grief of losing friends in India that the deceased must so soon be buried and out of sight.'

Every day they set themselves to preach and teach in the open air, using the advantage of huge, though hostile, crowds, at festival times. William Bampton and his wife made frequent, extended journeys into the interior of Orissa, barefoot and wearing native dress, since it made fording rivers and crossing swamps more practicable. They were heard but mocked, as they struggled with the language.

'The Oriya is a hard language to speak,' Sutton observed ruefully at the end of a long day, 'and shouting to a large company in it for two or three hours is very hard labour.'

Life in Cuttack, where there was a European community, and where the missionaries established schools, an orphanage and in 1826 a chapel of whitewashed brick with a thatched roof and a verandah, was tolerable. Life at Puri, within sight and sound of the temple, was a constant onslaught on the feelings of Christian missionaries.

At the Bathing Festival and the Car Festival, the area was packed with pilgrims, many of them already half dead of exhaustion and hunger from their travels. Many of the lower castes were exploited and beaten by priests, while the East India Company itself exploited the situation in the Pilgrim Tax that appeared to offer official sanction to the horrors of Puri. As the giant idols, with grotesque faces, with bodies made from huge blocks of the nimb tree, with golden hands and feet, were dragged through the area on huge wheels with protruding spokes, pilgrims threw themselves beneath the wheels.

In the wake of such orgies of destruction, the Bamptons, Laceys and Amos Sutton, sometimes using money provided by more humane members of the government, moved among the piles of dead and dying, wounded and cholera-stricken wretches on the streets, holding out brandy and water here, gently carrying a broken body to hospital there, befriending an orphan here. When Peggs' ill health forced him to return to England, he was as Amos Sutton put it 'exhausted by sympathy with suffering humanity'. There lay – and lies – the dilemma of the missionary, predicted by John Thomas when he had said: 'Don't send to India men without feeling for they will do no good. Don't send men of feeling for they will soon die.'

In England Peggs urged the government to act against sati and against the Pilgrim Tax that had led Hindus to rebut the arguments of missionaries: 'If Juggernaut be nothing, why does the Company take so much money off the pilgrims at the entrance to the town?'

Meanwhile in Orissa in 1827 the mission rejoiced in the first baptism of a Hindu, Erun, a weaver. Their first real convert had been Gunga Dhor, a Brahman influenced by William Bampton's work in Berampur, but he had for several years hesitated to accept baptism. The missionaries understood that it was hard for a Brahman to be the first to break the chain of caste in the vicinity of Juggernaut. When he finally requested baptism, Gunga Dhor was taken to Cuttack because his life was threatened by his own community. In March 1829 he tore off his poita, the badge of his Brahmanhood, as he entered the water. His baptism was followed by that of his wife and he went on to be employed by the Society as a native preacher, his first convert being a Brahman woman.

It was, as Amos Sutton described it, 'uphill work'. The Orissa missionaries experienced a cultural loneliness probably greater than anything ever known at Serampore. Their converts too faced cruel isolation, their wives and families often disowning them, the barber refusing to shave them, the washerwoman to wash their clothes, yet in the most idolatrous area of India the claims of Christ had begun to be heard.

*

Carey died in June 1834, three years before the rift between Serampore and London was formally ended in the Act of Reunion signed at Fen Court in the presence of John Mack in December 1837. Although, as Ward had predicted, the relationship with the younger missionaries had been healed, the past two decades had been darkened not only by the controversy with the home committee but by a series of deaths that had left the community at Serampore aching and sorrowful.

Charlotte, who had in her spirituality, intelligence and gift for languages been a kindred spirit of a wife for William, died in 1821. Krishna Pal, a valued missionary in early work in Jessore, in Dinajpur and in reconnaisance work in Dacca, died of cholera in 1822. The same year Felix Carey died of fever at the age of thirty-seven and then one year later in a further cruel blow, William Ward, busy training the more advanced students at Serampore College for missionary work, succumbed to cholera.

Economic blows, too, fell thick and fast. Flood devastated part of the Serampore site including Carey's home. Financial retrenchment in India as the result of war with Burma in 1825 meant that Carey's Fort William professorship was discontinued. A series of crashes in Calcutta banks robbed the mission of money lodged there just as it was needed for the work spreading out into several areas of Bengal and hit, too, the parents of students at the mission's schools and colleges.

Yet, amidst so much sadness, there was cause for satisfaction too. John Mack, who shared the college house with Carey, proved a source of great comfort and strength to him and became in 1832 joint pastor of the Serampore Church with Carey and Marshman. In his academic work he was joined by John Leechman, a graduate of Glasgow University, and by John C. Marshman.

The church at Lall Bazar flourished under the pastorate of William Robinson, who had returned to Calcutta after hard, lonely and unrewarding work in Bhutan, in Java and in Sumatra, and the death of two wives. He had, as a fellow missionary observed, been 'enough driven about in the world', but in Lall Bazar he found fulfilment and from the Lall Bazar church a steady stream of missionary recruits flowed out into the scattered work in Bengal.

It was indeed scattered and difficult work. The second Baptist church in Bengal had been founded at Dinajpur. Carey's time there, though brief, had resulted in the conversion of an influential merchant, Ignatius Fernandez. Baptized at Serampore, Fernandez then returned to Dinajpur for thirty years of faithful missionary work which, however, foundered after his death.

Work in Jessore suffered from diffuseness and from the fact that it was hard to care for and to follow up new converts. An experiment in forming a 'Christian village', where outcasts could live together, was a response to the real problem of how to sustain new Christians rejected by their community with the loss of caste, work and home. In terms of Christian witness, however, it was not a promising solution, for it intensified the isolation of Christians, and so it was abandoned.

In the opening decades of the century, work amongst Buddhist Arakene Burmese people living in the Chittagong area flourished but was severely set back by the war between India and Burma.

Several reconnaissance trips by boat into the area round Dacca, much of it inaccessible except by water, led to sustained work in education in Dacca by Mr Leonard, a former soldier with the East India Company, who had become a member of the Lall Bazar church. He established schools for nominally Roman Catholic children of Portuguese fathers and Indian mothers, while Ram Prasad, Carey's first Brahman convert, joined him as an evangelist. After two decades of dogged work there, Leonard's place was taken by William Robinson, who worked in Dacca until his death eighteen years later.

Meanwhile a very young man, John Smith, left with a full load of Scriptures in his boat for Barisal, to be joined there by brother Parry, a more senior member of the Lall Bazar church.

So, never with sustained success, in an area both geographically and spiritually inhospitable, by often inexperienced and all too fallible men, began work in what is now Bangladesh. The Association of Baptist Churches in Bengal was formed in 1843.

In Colombo in Ceylon, a predominantly Buddhist country, a small church was founded by James Chater, helped by his first convert, a young Dutchman named Sies. To Chater's years of struggle was added personal tragedy. His two eldest sons, sent to England in 1815, drowned when their ship went down. When Ann Chater's health broke down, she too set off for England with the remaining family but died on the way. Perhaps it was fitting that James also died at sea on his way to England in 1828.

He had, however, achieved the translation of the New Testament into Sinhalese, continuing the tradition of translation work that has always characterized Baptist missionary work in the Indian subcontinent. Later in the century the Rev. Charles Chater was to produce the English/Sinhalese dictionary that is still the basis for modern dictionaries. Gottlob Bruckner, a German who went to India with the London Missionary Society but then became a Baptist, translated the New Testament into Javanese, though Baptist Missionary Society work in Java ended in 1847.

So the first three or four decades of the nineteenth century were marked in India by personal tragedy yet willing sacrifice, by human inexperience and fallibility yet by great intellectual achievement, and by a diffuseness born of an understandable urge to spread the good news ever further.

3. Free Indeed

Jamaica 1824 to 1870

It was a warm, still morning in early June 1832. Haze hung over the skyline of the fast-growing city of Liverpool. Only the gentlest of waves lapped the ship that lay outside it waiting to be taken up the Mersey.

A tall, strong passenger, his skin tanned by eight years in the West Indies, watched with barely concealed impatience as the pilot came on board.

'Well, pilot, what news?' William Knibb wanted to know. It was a mark of the raised political consciousness of the time that there was just one item of news in the forefront of the pilot's mind.

'The Reform Bill is passed.'

Few inhabitants of Liverpool could fail to have hopes for the Reform Act. The city's docks were busy with the cotton trade, its railway link with Manchester just completed by George Stephenson, yet its streets and alleys were darkened by poverty and overcrowding in slums where later that day the air would be foetid and the sunshine would hardly penetrate. Now the Reform Act was to extend the vote to many more people, especially in the middle classes and in urban areas, and make Members of Parliament more accountable to their constituents. It was, the people hoped, good news for Liverpool. And for Knibb?

'Thank God,' was the missionary's response. 'Now I'll have slavery down. I will never rest, day or night, till I see it destroyed, root and branch.'

The hatred of slavery that burst from William Knibb into

the stillness of an English summer evening was not unique to him. It was the struggles of Wilberforce, Granville Sharp and Clarkson that had culminated in the abolition of the slave trade throughout the British Empire in 1807. Many nonconformist Christians, including John Wesley, the Baptist Robert Hall, and John Ryland who in his college at Bristol was preparing many men for mission overseas, supported that struggle.

It had been hoped that, if the trade in captured Africans were stopped, slave owners would have to pay more attention to conserving life amongst the slaves they already worked. Such hopes of a lessening of cruelty in the sugar plantations of the West Indies had been short-lived. In 1823 a new generation of campaigners, led by the Quaker Thomas Buxton, had formed the Anti-Slavery Society. Since then the struggle between those who wanted a complete end to slavery and the strong West India party had rent Parliament. Was William Knibb right in his hopes that the extension of the vote through the Reform Act would now produce a Parliament more sympathetic to the cause? To the cause that throbbed in his pulses as the ship was eased gently into her berth?

For Knibb was a man with a mission. In 1824 he had sailed with a mission to Jamaica, aboard *The Ocean*, the same ship that had taken his brother to the West Indies just a few months previously. Thomas, like John Rowe, who had gone to Jamaica in 1812 to build on work started by emancipated Negro slaves from America, Moses Baker and George Liele, had died within months.

William had now survived eight years, forming a Jamaica Baptist Association together with his missionary colleagues, Coultart and Tinson at Kingston, Phillippo at Spanish Town, Phillips at Anatra Bay, Burchell at Montego Bay. Evocative names for a beautiful turtle-shaped island of wooded blue mountains, valleys and savannahs, pale beaches and sparkling sea. But now it was an island seething with hatred and misery and Knibb had a new mission. Not to Jamaica but from it. To tell it how it was.

He did not linger in Liverpool. A stage coach took him, via Kettering, the birthplace of the Society and his own birthplace too, to London.

In the BMS office at Fen Court, the committee awaited Knibb's arrival with unease. The Secretary John Dyer, embroiled in the dispute with Serampore, was in no mood for further controversy. When the Society had chosen Jamaica as its second field in the early part of the century, it had been clear about the role of the missionaries. They were to preach the Gospel within the social system there and to remain politically uninvolved. Dyer himself had spelt the policy out clearly to William Knibb.

'You are quite aware,' he had cautioned him, 'that the state of society in Jamaica is very different from that under which it is our privilege to live in this country, and that the great majority of its inhabitants are dependent upon their superiors in a degree altogether unknown here. The evidences of the fact will probably, especially at first, be painful and trying to your feelings; but you must ever bear in mind that, as a resident in Jamaica, you have nothing whatever to do with its civil and political affairs; and with these you must never interfere . . .'

For all these warnings, disturbing news had been reaching England from Jamaica. There was good news, yes, of the Christian faith spreading rapidly amongst the slave population, of schools opened and chapels built. But there were also unsettling stories of animosity between the missionaries and the sugar planters and of unrest amongst the slaves stirred up, it was alleged, by Baptists, The BMS committee had thought that they perhaps needed words with Phillippo, Burchell and Knibb. But they had hardly expected the missionaries to seize the initiative by sending Knibb to see *them*. And, as was immediately apparent, in no mood for compromise.

William Knibb was energetic, warm-hearted and resolute. He had been sent by his colleagues in Jamaica with a mission. A committee in Fen Court urging prudence was not going to stand in his way.

'Myself, my wife and my children,' he acknowledged, 'are entirely dependent on the Baptist mission; we have landed without a shilling, and may at once be reduced to penury. But, if it be necessary, I will take them by the hand, and walk bare-foot through the kingdom, but I will make known to the Christians of England what their brethren in Jamaica are suffering.'

So what had happened over the past eight years to render William Knibb at once so passionate and so resolute? Like his colleagues, he *had* arrived in Jamaica, intent simply on preaching the Gospel. He had fully intended to follow Dyer's advice, indeed had done so with a patient doggedness all the more remarkable in one so spirited.

But what the missionaries had found in Jamaica had horrified them. As high-principled men, who took their young wives with them, they were offended by the moral laxity of the planters who ran the estates, often managers in the absence of owners squandering time and money in the high life of English society.

And they were appalled at the cruelty meted out to the slaves, often women and children, who worked the estates. For the most trivial offences, slaves could be manacled and forced to work in chains, flogged, threatened with eviction from the pathetic huts in which they lived on the estates. John Dyer had warned William Knibb that he might find the system – what was it? – 'trying to his feelings'. What Knibb in fact felt was 'a burning hatred of slavery'. And shame. 'I feel ashamed,' he said as day after day his eyes were opened to the reality of life in Jamaica, 'to belong to a race that indulges in such atrocities.'

Life for the Negro was a weary catalogue of bad news. It was hardly surprising, therefore, that the slaves should respond swiftly and wholeheartedly to the good news brought to them by the missionaries.

'The poor, oppressed and deprived sons of Africa,' Knibb reported, 'form a pleasing contrast to the debauched white population. They gladly hear the word and to them the Gospel is preached.'

James Phillippo, Thomas Burchell and William Knibb had arrived in Jamaica within months of each other, setting up stations at Spanish Town, Montego Bay and Savanna-la-Mar. Not surprisingly, the planters felt threatened by men very different from the clergy of the Established Church; men who preached the God-endowed value of every human being and who set about teaching Negroes to read and write.

For two years, Phillippo, working in Spanish Town, at that time the capital of the island, was refused a licence to preach. He was arrested for refusing to do military service. He was harassed for baptizing slaves without their owners' permission. Yet still the Negroes came to hear, and dawn over the island often saw daybreak prayer meetings of between 600 and 1000 slaves.

The missionaries and their people erected chapels, only to find them bursting at the seams. 'Last Sabbath,' Phillippo told his colleagues, 'there were more hearers outside than within.' A passionate believer in the importance of education, Phillippo set up Sunday schools and day schools, drawing many of the Jewish population of the town.

In response to the opportunities, the missionaries took on workloads that would have taxed the health of men in a more comfortable climate. It was a weary Phillippo who, aware that he must find time to keep his friends in England up to date, put pen to paper one sultry November evening.

'Having preached three times yesterday,' he wrote, 'and occupied two hours in each service, I feel very tired. Had it been otherwise, I should have sent you an account of a baptizing at Old Harbour on the Sabbath before last. I administered that ordinance to ninety-five persons in the presence of, I suppose, a thousand spectators, and then preached out of doors, on a chair, soon after, to a congregation of the same number. On the following morning Mr Taylor accompanied me to another parish, about sixteen miles from Old Harbour and twenty-seven from Spanish Town, where we have succeeded in forming a new station, not likely to be of any expense to the Society.'

So, in events dramatically different from those in India, spread the Gospel in Jamaica. Slaves who had had to learn patient submission to cruel masters now gladly offered patient submission to a loving Lord. Often they had something to teach their pastors. Early in their time in Jamaica, Hannah and James Phillippo had a stillborn child, their third baby in succession to die. Their Negro people came to comfort them.

'Dear minister, don't grieve so much,' they begged him. 'Don't you often tell us that it is wrong to sorrow as those without hope, and that we must thank God for all things: God is too good to us poor sinners. What minister do, if God take missus, and left the child?'

Were the planters justified in feeling threatened by the work of the Baptist missionaries and the growth of the churches? If they had really had eyes to see, they would have recognized that the slaves connected with the Baptist churches were in fact more orderly and peaceable and more disposed to work than before.

Yet, alarmed by events in the island and by noises from England where Buxton was beavering away in the

Commons, the Jamaican Assembly passed a Consolidated Slave Law, never in fact to be ratified by the British Government. Slaves were not to preach or teach without their owners' permission; religious meeting houses were to be closed between sunset and sunrise; religious teachers were not to take money from slaves.

These were measures clearly aimed at the Baptists, though there were also Methodist missionaries working in the island. The building of the chapels and schools had been helped by the financial offerings of the Negroes themselves, who now found other uses than drink for what money they had. Slaves who worked ten hours in the fields had little opportunity for daytime worship. And what did 'teaching and preaching' embrace? Sam Swiney, a deacon of William Knibb's church, was soon to find out.

With a few other people, Sam came to pray at the home of his pastor, who was sick. A magistrate, informed of this, insisted that 'preaching and praying are the same thing'. Knibb, who had brought Sam the news of a Saviour to whom he could take everything in prayer and also of a truth that could set him free, watched as his deacon received twenty lashes on his back and was immediately dragged to his feet to work in chains on the roads.

What were Knibb and his colleagues to do? What were they to tell their people about the use of Sunday? It was all very well for a committee in England to draw up a policy. The missionaries were harassed, slandered and, with 10,000 church members and 17,000 enquirers for half a dozen or so ministers, physically and spiritually tired. Knibb, now minister at Falmouth, wrote to John Dyer, desperate for advice.

'One of the inquirers here was this day threatened with flogging and imprisonment for not standing in the market all Lord's day to sell her master's goods . . . I have told them not to obey their owners in this respect, as it is contrary to the laws of God, and to those of the land. How would you act? Let me know. We really need instructions on these points.'

Suddenly events in Jamaica moved swiftly. For some time the island had been buzzing with rumour. The anti-slavery campaign in England stung the planters into preparing for the defence of their system. At public meetings and in their masters' own homes, slaves overheard threats about the resistance the planters would offer to any move toward emancipation. Sometimes the planters directly taunted the slaves.

'Freedom is coming from England,' they jeered, 'but I shall shoot every damned black rascal of mine before he gets it.'

If the idea spread that freedom was decreed by the British Parliament but being withheld by the planters, only one section of the community was to blame. Not the slaves and not the missionaries, who were at pains to disabuse the slaves of the idea and to urge patience and restraint. Yet the idea got about that James Burchell, who was in England trying to restore his health damaged by the Jamaican climate and his workload there, would on his return to the island be bringing the 'free papers'.

As Christmas 1831 approached, a passive resistance movement was born, led by a Baptist deacon, Sam Sharp. At meetings on an estate called Reprieve, some of the slaves decided that after Christmas they would peaceably refuse to work any longer without pay. When the planters curtailed the Christmas holidays, however, a spark was set to the timber of rumour and resentment. On 27th December, sugar works blazed as some of the slaves were swept into insurrection. Their gesture was inevitably short-lived, swiftly and cruelly crushed. Four hundred Negroes were killed by the militia, 100 were hanged or shot and a further 100 flogged, some to death.

Then the planters turned their attention to the missionaries. Knibb, arrested with his colleagues Abbott and Whitehorne, was perhaps not surprised. 'No fault had I committed,' he reflected, 'with none was I charged. But I was a missionary and that was enough.'

The three men were taken by boat from Falmouth to Montego Bay, seven hours in an open canoe under a blazing sun. Held at bayonet-point in the court-house, it was a moot point who would have killed them first, the soldiers inside or the mob outside, had an influential friend not come to their rescue with bail. On 7th January Thomas Burchell sailed into Montego Bay on the *Garland Grove*, knowing nothing of recent events and the martial law that had been imposed. Looking forward to a reunion with his people, he found himself instead imprisoned on the frigate *Blanche*.

Twice the missionaries were freed and rearrested as the planters searched desperately for evidence and witnesses against them. Frustrated, they turned their attention instead to the chapels and mission houses. On 7th February the chapel at Falmouth blazed. In the following few days the chapels at Stewart Town, Morant Bay, Brown's Town and Savanna-la-Mar were razed to the ground.

Freed, the missionaries found their congregations scattered, their chapels in ruins, their homes destroyed and their own lives so threatened that only their bravest friends could offer shelter to them and their families. The planters had formed the Colonial Church Union, aimed at controlling the clergy themselves and driving Dissenters from the island. It was now clear that slavery could not exist side by side with Christian missions. The planters, for the sake of maintaining the system of slavery, were ready violently to expel Christianity. Burchell, for his own safety, was persuaded to leave for America for a while. But the other missionaries had no intention of being forced from their work. It was time for Knibb's visit to England.

*

On the platform of the Exeter Hall in London, a pair of slave shackles was hurled to the floor. The crash was followed by a stunned silence that would later give way to thunderous applause. William Knibb, freed himself from the restraints that had bound him for eight years, had begun his campaign. And he was a passionate and eloquent speaker.

With the blessing of the committee, touched by his words at Fen Court, he had spoken to the autumn meeting of the Baptist Missionary Society in Spa Fields Chapel. Phillippo, in England for his health, had joined him there, detailing the work of the mission. Knibb had spoken about slavery, his words simple but directed at the deepest principles of his hearers.

'I plead for liberty to worship God on behalf of 30,000 Christians of the same faith as yourselves . . .' he told them. 'I plead on behalf of the widows and orphans of those whose innocent blood has been shed . . . I plead on behalf of my brethren in Jamaica, whose hopes are fixed on this meeting. I plead on behalf of their wives and their little ones. I call upon children by the cries of the infant slave whom I saw flogged on Macclesfield estate, in Westmorland parish.'

Now, on 15th August, Knibb had moved his platform to a public meeting at the Exeter Hall. Again his case was simple but heart-stirring.

'Having been sent here to vindicate my African brethren and the religious society with which I stand connected, I disclaim all political feeling in the performance of that duty. I look upon the question of slavery only as one of religion and morality. All I ask is that my African brother may stand in the family of man; that my African sister shall, while she clasps her tender infant to her breast, be allowed to call it her own; that they both shall be allowed to bow their knees in prayer to that God who has made of one blood all nations.'

From that meeting onwards and for the rest of the year, Knibb was in a state of perpetual motion. Sometimes accompanied by Burchell who had arrived from America, he toured England and Scotland with his irrefutable message. From Bristol to Norwich, from Newcastle to Cornwall, in Scotland and in Northern Ireland, he moved hundreds of thousands of people to tears and to outrage. He withstood the attacks of the press and of West India party hecklers planted in his meetings. He appeared before committees of both houses of Parliament. And now the time was right. His hopes on that summer morning in Liverpool had been well founded, for the election following the passing of the Reform Act had returned many MPs pledged to the abolition of slavery. With Knibb provoking outcry up and down the land, Earl Grey was forced to resolve the issue once and for all.

On 14th May 1833, the Colonial Secretary, Edward Stanley, proposed the abolition of slavery, pointing to the conviction of the people of the country that 'things wrong in principle cannot be expedient in practice'. He introduced 'An Act for the abolition of slavery throughout the British colonies, for promoting the industry of the emancipated slave, and for compensating the persons hitherto entitled to their services'.

The final clause was amply executed. £20,000,000 compensation was voted to slave holders. Of more concern to the campaigners, however, was that a system of 'apprenticeship' with the slaves still working for the planters, was to last for six years prior to full emancipation. The Government hoped that this interim period would afford time for legislation, social reform and education to prepare the Negroes for full freedom. Phillippo, who knew the planters better than the English Parliament, feared that they would take the opportunity to wring the last drop of blood from the system.

The royal assent was given to the bill on 28th August. William Knibb longed with all his heart to be back with his people. Now, with the Sunday markets closed, they were free to gather on the Lord's Day. But there was no chapel in Falmouth or in dozens of places on the island where once the mission stations had been flourishing. His work in England was not done. It was not done until, having elicited £12,000 compensation from the British Government, the BMS itself raised £13,000 to rebuild the chapels.

On 25th October 1834, William, Mary and their small children sailed into Port Maria. The planters who had vowed that he would never return to Jamaica watched with mute but burning resentment as his people welcomed him home with an avalanche of joy.

*

The treadmill under the blazing Jamaican sun was moving too fast for the pregnant Negro woman who repeatedly missed her step. Her punishment for that was to be tied to the wheel and flogged. This was 'apprenticeship'. This was the period that the British Government had hoped would be used positively to prepare the Negroes for freedom.

'I think nearly forty young and old females pass my door in chains every morning,' William Knibb observed in mingled despair and fury. 'Not one school is yet established, whilst most abominable cells and treadmills are being erected all over the place! This to prepare the poor things for freedom!'

Phillippo's prediction had been right. Before emancipation could come, the planters intended to use the apprenticeship system to work the Negroes to death. The apprentices, working forty-five hours a week without pay for their masters, found it impossible to save the money to buy their freedom, for the price put on them was higher now than when they had been slaves. Special magistrates, appointed to administer justice to the apprentices, found the work-house and the treadmill to be new ways of meting out vicious punishments.

Letters were again flying backward and forward between the West Indies and England, where accounts of the cruelty were often assumed to be exaggerated.

'I know you wish me to be quiet,' Knibb wrote to John Dyer, 'but I cannot. Place yourself in my situation and I think you would act too. I hope I shall never live to see the day when I can behold a bleeding, chained Christian female and fail to defend her through fear of men.'

In the Jamaican House of Assembly, Lord Sligo, appointed as Governor to carry out the Emancipation Act, tried in vain to force the planters into a semblance of humanity. Bitterly (he was later to resign in despair, to be replaced by Sir Lionel Smith) he detailed to them their own obduracy:

'I pressed on you the establishment of more Courts of Assizes, so strongly recommended by the presentment of the Grand Jury. You took no notice of it . . . The whipping of females, you were informed by me, officially, was in practice; and I called on you to make enactments to put an end to conduct so repugnant to humanity and so contrary to law. So far from passing an Act to prevent the recurrence of such cruelty, you have in no way expressed your disapprobation of it . . . I informed you that £25,000 sterling had been voted by England for the support of education in the colonies, with the promise of still further assistance being afforded, and you have taken no steps to make it available.'

There were, of course, some fair-minded planters but the

majority were against them. But, if the planters had no intention of providing education for the apprentices, the missionaries redoubled their efforts to do so. New schools were opened and James Phillippo obtained 1500 copies of Scripture from the Bible Societies for apprentices who could read and ran two libraries for the use of his congregation.

Teaching the new Christians was a massive task for, despite the fact that Baptist apprentices were often the target of particularly vicious punishment on any pretext, the churches continued to grow. The missionaries were overworked and stressed, a situation not helped by criticism from England that their churches were inadequately supervised. What, Phillippo wanted to know, were the overstretched missionaries supposed to do?

'If the churches in Jamaica are inferior to those in England in piety and sound Scriptural knowledge, what has been the cause and who are to blame? Not the missionaries and their flocks but British Christians, in so scantily supplying the field with labourers. I, for instance, have a church amounting to nearly 1500 members, with perhaps an equal or a greater number of inquirers . . . I can, therefore, scarcely be supposed to perform so many pastoral visits, or to possess so many opportunities for communicating private instruction, as a pastor at home, who has less than one-third of such duties to perform.'

But perhaps the most significant letter of all was written by John Clarke, minister at Brown's Town, to Joseph Sturge, a corn-merchant in Birmingham, a Quaker and the leader of the younger members of the Anti-Slavery Society. Invited to see the apprenticeship system at work for himself, Joseph Sturge came out to Jamaica with Thomas Harvey.

Not only did they return to England to publish an account of their findings entitled *The West Indies in 1837*.

They took with them John Williams, an apprentice whose freedom they had purchased, and who was ready to describe the floggings, the imprisonment and the hours on the treadmill he had suffered.

Once again England was in uproar. Leaders in the press, petitions to the Prime Minister and the Commons demanded the abolition of the apprenticeship system on the grounds that the planters had violated the contract. Overtaken by events of their own making, the Jamaica Assembly conceded that on 1st August 1838 all 300,000 Negroes should be free.

William and Mary Knibb, often sought out by oppressed people, had had personal sorrows of their own during the previous turbulent year. Their son, Thomas, named after their friend Burchell, had died in 1836. His younger brother William became the object of his father's hopes, for he had been brought up to hate slavery with a passion like his father's and to share his father's dream that the Negroes might one day take the Gospel back to Africa. William died of fever shortly before the slaves whose misery had stirred him were finally free. So that, on 1st August 1838, only one thing marred William's joy. 'Oh! had my boy, my lovely slavery-hating boy been there!'

As congregations gathered in every chapel across the island, the Negroes arriving for worship at Falmouth at 11.00 p.m. on 31st July found a huge banner bearing the word 'Freedom' across the entrance to the chapel. Knibb counted every last second till midnight and, as the final stroke died away, cried with all the fervour and relief of the bitter struggle finally won: 'The monster is dead! The Negro is free!'

In the small hours of the morning, in the grounds of the Suffield Schoolroom, a grave was dug and a coffin lowered into Jamaica soil. In it had been placed the instruments dreaded by the slaves – a chain, a whip, an iron collar. Over it was hung the flag of freedom with the Union Jack in its corner.

*

In the mountains above Spanish Town, James Phillippo walked with an unquiet mind. Many times in the years leading up to emancipation, when the heat and bustle of the town had sapped his physical strength and made clamorous inroads into his spiritual energy, these mountains had beckoned him with their promise of peace. Just five years ago, this area had been nothing but a wilderness of rock and untamed vegetation, to which time and again he had come with relief to stare out over a shimmering sea.

But now this was a wilderness transformed. The chatter of children came from a row of cottages on his left. Negro mothers, no longer forced to labour long hours in the fields, played with their babies. Phillippo waved to women in gardens claimed from the undergrowth, women whose weddings he had conducted in the tidal wave of marriages that had followed the slaves' freedom to marry. He could see the husbands and fathers working in the fields of sugar-cane and fruit that stretched away down the hillside.

At the end of the row of cottages, he gently pushed open the door of the chapel and let himself into the cool dimness. This had been the first building erected in Sligoville, the heart of the community. He had come here now with an uneasy spirit to reassure himself that all was well.

Yes, surely in 1843 all was well in Jamaica. The years following emancipation had, not surprisingly, for no preparation had been made for them, been hard. The planters had needed labourers; the people had needed work and shelter. But on whose terms and at what price? When many of the planters had offered miserly wages and exorbitant rents for the huts on the estates, the missionaries had had to negotiate where possible on behalf of the Negroes and to urge justice and commonsense.

'Take time to consider the subject,' William Knibb had urged the Negroes who sought him out for advice. 'If you demand too high a wage the planters will be ruined: if you consent to take too low a sum you will not be able to provide for the wants of yourselves and your families.'

But as compromise often proved impossible, and as many of the estates were abandoned or broken up as planters decided to take the liberal compensation provided by the British Government and leave the island, Phillippo and his colleagues had seen another way forward. With the help of wealthy well-wishers in England, they had bought up land and offered it as smallholdings to the Negroes, forming free townships.

Sligoville had been one of the first townships but now almost 200 new communities, covering a total of 100,000 acres offered secure homes and work to thousands of Negro families. Their names – Sturge Town, Granville, Wilberforce, Buxton, Clarkstonville – were a tribute to those who had befriended the Negro in the struggle for freedom. But the peaceful industry that surrounded Phillippo as he sat in the quiet chapel was a tribute to the character of the Negroes themselves and the Christian faith that many of them had found.

'When I reflect upon the circumstance that 300,000 human beings have been set free in this island,' William Knibb had said, 'and that not one of them has ever raised his hand to strike a white man, I cannot but rejoice that the moral influence of religion has been so manifest.'

Twenty-four new recruits, sent by the BMS to Jamaica between 1839 and 1842, had founded eighteen new churches, nineteen new schools and twenty-three new mission houses, generously supported by church members who had much for which to be thankful. The Society itself was hard put to find money for the rapid extension of the work in the West Indies while fulfilling its commitments in India and tentatively exploring the possibility of mission in West Africa urged on it by William Knibb. So Phillippo had not been surprised when a suggestion by the Jamaica Baptist Assembly that from the 1st August 1842 they should be financially independent of the home society, had been welcomed in London.

The Jamaica Baptist Assembly had in fact formed its own missionary society, working in Haiti, Cuba, Panama and the Bahamas. In the face of urgent need to train Negro Christians to be pastors of the growing churches, they had also opened Calabar College, under the Presidency of Joshua Timson, who in seven years laid a foundation that 'Father' David East was to build on for forty. Everything seemed to be humming as busily and contentedly as the insects that kept an incessant murmur in the flowers outside the door of the chapel in Sligoville.

Yet Phillippo was uneasy. He alone had doubted the wisdom of the break – financial independence meant autonomy in other senses as well – from the home society. The new buildings had incurred heavy debts, which might not be paid off for many years even if all continued to go well with Jamaica. And what if it did not?

*

In the event, the catalogue of misery that overtook Jamaica over the next twenty years could not have been foreseen by Phillippo, uneasy though he was about the debts of the churches. It was caused by factors partly outside the control of those on the island. In Britain, the Government, having repealed the Corn Laws, moved towards a policy of Free Trade, that in effect placed agriculture behind industry in importance and both behind trade. Favourable duties had given the West Indies a virtual monopoly of the sugar trade with England. Their removal struck at the lifeblood of the islands.

To economic damage was added natural disaster in the form of a series of droughts and epidemics. As Phillippo moved in 1850 round the cholera-stricken homes of Spanish Town, his peaceful moments in the chapel at Sligoville were no more than a mocking memory. His colleagues and confidants, Knibb and Burchell, were now dead and it was to the lonely pages of his diary that he spelled out the events of one Sunday.

'Called at several houses. Saw several persons dead and dying. Called at the hospital and found more dead there and the hospital in a filthy state. Preached to a thin congregation, owing to the great mortality in the neighbourhood. Called again at the hospital and ordered a nurse to be procured . . . The Farm Pen, the property of Lord Carrington, was rapidly decimating; several had been interred without coffins, and numbers were being taken with the epidemic every hour. I prayed with all the patients and returned to town at dark.'

Twenty thousand people in three months, and eventually one tenth of the population, were to die of cholera. Agricultural work on the island came to a standstill. The debts on the mission buildings, confidently assumed in more hopeful days, now appeared as crippling burdens. The stipends of the ministers also had to be found. Spiritual revival in the early 1860s could not alter the economic straits of the people. Twice the BMS made grants to the Jamaican churches and twice it sent delegations to see for themselves the difficulties on the island.

Dyer had died in tragic circumstances in 1841, leaving the young Joseph Angus to work away at the relationship with Serampore, to preside over the Jubilee Meetings of the Society in 1842 and to supervise a removal of headquarters from Fen Court to Moorgate. When Angus became President of Stepney College in 1849, Frederick Trestrail and Edward Underhill had replaced him as joint secretaries. It was Underhill who had special charge of the overseas fields and who in 1854 visited the stations in India, the first visit by a member of the home committee to that field in all its sixty years. It was Underhill who visited Jamaica in 1857 and Underhill who in a sense precipitated the dramatic happenings of 1865 – happenings that were to be the culmination of Phillippo's fears for his beloved Jamaica and that were to change the course of events there.

Gone, by 1865, were the peaceful, prosperous scenes of industry in the townships. Instead, people sat idle and hungry – imported food and clothes too expensive for them to buy, crippling taxes even on the donkeys and carts they needed in order to work. The Jamaica Assembly was currupt and the Governor Eyre, as was to be proved, inept. Edward Underhill, moved by reports from the missionaries of the plight of the people, wrote to Cardwell, the Colonial Secretary, urging intervention and help.

That letter was passed to Governor Eyre who allowed it to become public knowledge. He asked the 'costos' and clergy of each area to provide their own assessment of the situation. The people felt that it was time to make their own voice heard, and did so at a series of meetings which became known as 'Underhill Meetings' throughout the island.

Once again, as in the not-forgotten days of 1831, the island was buzzing with a heightened excitement and resentment that needed but one spark to set it ablaze. When James Phillippo, in common with his fellow ministers, was asked to pin up in his area the 'Queen's Advice', his heart lurched as he recognized the danger. The two placards, purporting to be advice from the Queen to the people of Jamaica, assured them that, far from outside intervention being necessary, all that was needed to ensure their prosperity was their own prudence and industry. The missionaries refused to publish the placard but, across the island, the damage had been done and the spark ignited.

At Morant Bay, in the extreme south-east of the island, a group of Negroes seeking to air their grievances at the court-house on 8th October were fired on by troops. The riot that ensued was put down with vicious retribution. Hundreds of Negroes were rounded up to be flogged and executed; a thousand homes were razed to the ground. A Royal Commission set up by the British Government to replace Eyre and to enquire into the bloody events stated categorically and baldy: 'The punishments inflicted were excessive. The floggings were reckless. The burning of a thousand homes was wanton and cruel.'

How deep ran the resentments of the past fifty years. But now at last there was help for Jamaica and encouragement for the missionaries who had spent themselves there. Sir John Grant, the new Governor, instituted a new Legislative Council. He set up district courts with magistrates from England prepared to ensure justice for the people. Though he could not undo decades of economic damage, he applied taxes more fairly. And, gladdening the heart of the elderly missionary who had so prized education, he introduced a system of elementary education for the whole population. He provided also a new missionary challenge. Grant himself suggested that mission stations be set up in the Morant Bay area and the BMS responded with money for staff and buildings.

The achievements of fifty years of Christian mission in Jamaica were unfolding into new opportunities. But yet another challenge had by now presented itself to the BMS. It had all begun on a day in 1843 when William Knibb had steered out of Falmouth harbour the sailing ship *Chilmark*, bound for Fernando Po.

4. Africa for Christ

Africa 1840 to 1914

For William Knibb, it was the fulfilment of a dream. Nine years earlier he had said that 'If my labours are so blessed to the sons of Africa as to cause them to go forth to their countrymen with the glad tidings of salvation, then I shall think that Africa is about to be repaid for all her wrongs.'

For the BMS, it was the second stage in a process that had begun three years earlier in 1840 when they had sent John Clarke, formerly a missionary in Jamaica, and Dr George Prince, one-time plantation owner, to report on the prospects of work in Fernando Po in the Bight of Biafra. For this was the century of European penetration of Africa, stretching from James Bruce's Ethiopian journey in 1768 to the death of Livingstone in 1873.

And for the forty-two Jamaicans packed on board the *Chilmark*, it was the start of a venture of faith, to take the Gospel that had come to mean so much to them back to their West African homeland. They had responded to the cry for help from Clarke and Prince, who *en route* from Fernando Po to England to make their favourable report, had been blown off course, providentially as it seemed, to Jamaica. And now, as promised, the *Chilmark* had come for them, led by Joseph Merrick, formerly pastor of the church at Jericho, and Alexander Fuller, a Spanish Town carpenter. Fifteen hundred members of the Jamaican churches had gathered at Falmouth for a Communion service and to wish them 'God speed'.

Their hopes were so high that they were able to ignore the

cramped conditions aboard the sailing vessel of just 179 tons and even the obvious disdain of the captain and crew for the Negro passengers. Alfred Saker, who had left his work at Devonport dockyard when he heard the first-hand accounts of Clarke and Prince, was incensed on their behalf. As the *Chilmark* progressed agonizingly slowly across the Atlantic, he was anxious too for his pregnant wife.

Seldom could a couple have been more equally yoked for missionary work than Alfred and Helen. He was the son of a Kent millwright and engineer. He had little formal education, yet he proved as Carey had done before him, that an impoverished background will not quench intellectual energy, an intellect that in his case delighted in things practical and scientific, in globes, telescopes, engines. Helen, before her marriage to Alfred, had already offered herself to the CMS. She had been turned down because missionary societies at that time did not send single women abroad.

Landfall at Fernando Po was made on 15th February 1844 and Helen's baby was born nine days later. They had come to a wooded, mountainous island 120 miles in circumference, lying almost opposite the mouth of the Cameroons river. Discovered by Portugal, it had been ceded to Spain in 1778 but abandoned four years later. Since 1827 Britain had used the township of Clarence on the north of the island as a base for its anti-slavery patrol. Many of the inhabitants were themselves freed slaves, making a living from servicing the needs of the ships that plied the coast. Here Clarke and Prince had started a small church, now in the care of the Sturgeons.

Despite work already begun, physical endurance was needed from the pioneers. A tornado threatened them the very day they arrived. White ants destroyed their wooden shelters almost as fast as they could build them. An acute shortage of food weakened them so that they succumbed quickly to dysentery. The baby girl born to the Sakers died within a few months, 'this first of the mission families that has fallen here', as Alfred put it, sensing surely the devastating toll of human life that was to mark the early years of mission in Africa.

Saker, a man of indomitable drive, who tolerated weakness no less in himself than in other people, was restless. The church at Clarence, under the pastorate of Sturgeon and then of Prince, was growing. The arrival of new recruits, few of them to survive long, gave Saker the opportunity he needed to turn his eyes to the mainland. Taking with him Horton Johnson, who was to prove one of the most faithful of the Jamaican workers, he sailed in the small schooner *Wasp* up the Cameroons river. The tribes of the area spoke a common language, Dualla, though that did not prevent repeated outbreaks of tribal warfare.

The settlement of Bethel began in a hut just 21 feet×15 feet granted to Saker by the area's king, less hostile than most of the Africans, who threatened and robbed Johnson and Saker and strewed their paths with the poisonous plants of their witchcraft. It was to the work at Bethel, where later a church was to be formed, that Saker gave his heart, though losses of staff at Clarence were repeatedly to necessitate his return to supervise the work on the island.

All Saker's experience at the mill and the shipyard came into its own at Bethel. He scrounged lead from passing ships to make a crude press, for he had started to translate the Scriptures into Dualla. As a counter-attack to the white ants, he taught African youths to make bricks from local clay, and over the years a chapel, storehouse and printing press were to be built at that 'house of God'.

When illness drove Helen and their child to England to recuperate, as it was to do many times, he threw himself more determinedly than ever into gruelling hard work. 'If I had nought to do,' he confessed, 'I should die of grief, so that my earnest cry every day is for an energy of spirit.'

If there was initially little response to preaching at Bethel, the battle against superstition and violence for Joseph Merrick at Bimbia was even harder. Yet Merrick translated Genesis and Matthew into the Isubu tongue and struggled on at Bimbia till death.

At Clarence, however, there were baptisms in the stream on New Year's Day 1848, and children flocked into the Sunday School. There was here both so much opportunity and what Saker called 'sorrow upon sorrow'. Leader after leader was taken by disease or death and many of the Jamaicans who had sailed with such high hopes in the *Chilmark*, returned home demoralized when Alexander Fuller, their natural leader, died. Yet Alexander's son, Joseph, remained to offer nearly forty years of faithful work in Africa.

For nearly three decades Alfred Saker dominated the work in West Africa, toiling like the man possessed that he undoubtedly was. What others might have called 'success' felt more like pain to him. 'We have three churches in as many different places,' he reported in 1852. 'We have two other places where the Word is regularly preached; yet what is the whole of this to the mass of men living in darkness around us? What proportion is a hundred members of churches to the tens of thousands treading the same soil, dancing before our eyes, alike careless of God and themselves?'

Spain, influenced by the Jesuits and by the great increase in trade in the Gulf of Guinea, revived her claim to Fernando Po and in 1858 proclaimed Roman Catholicism the only faith to be publicly professed there. Saker decided that it was time to find a new home for the community of Baptist Christians at Clarence. When, exploring the mainland coast, he came to Ambas Bay, a beautiful bay twenty miles long with an inlet two miles long to a sandy cove watered by a mountain stream, he knew he had found the site for 'Victoria'. 'Of this land,' acquired from the King of Bimbia, he reported to the home committee, 'we took possession with prayer.' For he and J. J. Fuller, who was to work there for many years, had a thoroughly Nonconformist vision for Victoria, 'a centre of freedom, of worship, of education and commerce'.

Saker's furloughs were partly to revive his health, for he was so exhausted and emaciated that his colleagues referred to him as 'the shadow', but partly to preserve his reputation with the home committee. As time went on and he gave much attention to the affairs of Victoria, there was dissension between him and his younger colleagues. It centred on the issue of the rôle of the missionary, a question to be raised repeatedly through two centuries. Building, agriculture, translating and printing were all very well to a point, the younger men argued, but not if it left little time for preaching, evangelism and theology.

Saker, who remembered the privations of the earliest years, and had seen how improvements in housing had decreased the rate of death and disease, saw things differently. To the BMS Secretary, Edward Underhill, sent from England to see the situation in the Cameroons for himself, Saker expressed himself in a way that we should probably consider ahead of his time.

'The true work of the missionary is, it seems, to go book in hand under a tree here and a shed there, and preach to the people. With me the work has ever appeared in a different light. It is to go to the man in his house, to sympathize in his sorrows and cares, to aid him to think of a better condition and of the means to attain it. Then, when his attention has been gained, to speak to him of that higher life which we have lost and which the loving hand of God will give us again if we will hear him. And what if such a lesson be given by showing a better way of planting and building? To me it has ever been that the spiritual work is to get at the heart of the individual man. How it is done I don't care a pin.'

In his strained relationships with his fellow missionaries, Saker was probably like Livingstone, who found it easier to get along with Africans than with his colleagues. Dissension drove him into autocratic silence and deeper into himself. Yet, loner that he was, his heart warmed as he watched the work of his daughter Emily. It was Emily who brought off the press the Dualla New Testament in 1862 and the Old Testament in 1868, printed by young Africans trained on the mission station. It was Emily who taught in the day school and ran meetings for women. And it was Emily who, shortly before her father's death, was accepted by the BMS as a missionary in her own right.

In his last days in Africa, 'the Shadow' cast longing eyes, as he had always done, toward the interior where Livingstone was making his last journeys. But Saker's work in Africa was also done. The BMS continued its work in the Cameroons until 1884 when it was handed over to the Basle mission, for Germany had assumed control of the Cameroons. When Saker came home to England for the last time, he left a young man called George Grenfell working with Jackson Fuller and at Sierra Leone he grasped the hand of Tom Comber *en route* for the Cameroons. But the spotlight was already shifting to a new area of Africa.

*

'Africa for Christ' was emblazoned across the cover of the *Missionary Herald* for September 1877. As the magazine found its way into churches and chapels in English towns and villages where 'Africa' had come to mean mineral wealth, rubber and David Livingstone, 'Africa for Christ' was echoed from the pulpit and the pew. Who could remain unmoved by the stories of how Stanley had found

Livingstone in 'darkest Africa' in November 1871 and had found, too, that the River Congo was an immense 4000 mile waterway right into the heart of Africa? And who, listening to Moody preach in his English campaign of 1875, could fail to be stirred to a new pitch of evangelical fervour?

Certainly not the young men who made up a good part of the average Baptist congregation in the late 1870s. Far from being 'enthusiastic' to be a 'dissenter' as it had been for Carey a century ago, it was now positively respectable to be an upright, hard-working, Victorian Nonconformist. The first administration of Gladstone had seen the abolition of the Religious Tests at Oxford, Cambridge and Durham, which had effectively excluded Nonconformists from university education. Now a new generation of intelligent young men had access to the universities, while other able young men trained for the family business. The young George Grenfell, growing up in Heanage Street Baptist Church in Birmingham, had been apprenticed to machinery merchants, while Tom Comber, baptized in Denmark Place Church in Camberwell, had been earmarked for his father's jewellery business until 'Africa for Christ' had become an irresistible call.

But the young men who worked in the family business during the day spent their evenings and Sundays at the church, the Bible class and the Sunday School that provided their social as well as their spiritual life and spent their Saturdays distributing tracts. They discussed their heroes, Livingstone and Saker, at Young Men's Missionary Societies, though it was to be thirty years or so before the Girls' Auxiliary of the Baptist Missionary Society, started in Glasgow in 1903, offered comparable meetings for young women.

'Africa for Christ' was far from being an exclusively Baptist vision. Other missionary societies had entered Africa from the east coast. The Free Church of Scotland was working at Lake Nyasa, the CMS in Uganda and the LMS at Lake Tanganyika. But the Baptists had their foothold on the west coast at the Cameroons, and from there first Saker and then Grenfell and Comber looked longingly inland. They shared the belief that the opportunities for missionary work amongst tribes on the coast had effectively been 'spoiled' by the demoralizing influence of traders. The way forward, in all senses, lay with people who were not yet resentful of, or corrupted and exploited by, the white man.

It was because the BMS was already working on the west coast and because it had proved itself to be 'evangelical' in its aims that the Society became the focus for the thoughts and prayers of a Quaker in Leeds. Robert Arthington was one son who did not follow into his father's business, for his father was a brewer and Robert was a man of strong principles.

Robert had read geography at Cambridge. He had devoured eagerly everything written about the journeys of Livingstone and Stanley. In his mind's eye he could almost see the scythe-shaped Congo river with its tributaries equalling its length again, its cataracts and its island shallows. He knew that at San Salvador the Portuguese had left a legacy of Roman Catholic influence but that now the churches there were crumbling away. Nothing – success, wealth, personal comfort, even food – mattered to him compared with his consuming passion that the Gospel should be taken to Africa. His friends watched as he became a 'miser for missions' and finally left him to what seemed to them his strange obsession. So it was from a bare and chilly home of chosen frugality that Robert Arthington wrote a letter that was to shape the work of the BMS for years to come.

'There is a part of Africa,' he wrote, 'not too far, I think from places where you have stations, on which I have long had my eye, with very strong desire that the blessing of the Gospel might be given to it. It is the Congo country – an old Kingdom, once possessed, indeed is now, of a measure of civilization, and to a limited extent instructed in the externals of the Christian religion . . . It is therefore a great satisfaction and a high and sacred pleasure to me to offer one thousand pounds, if the Baptist Missionary Society will undertake at once to visit these benighted, interesting people with the blessed light of the Gospel, teach them to read and write and give them in imperishable letters the words of eternal truth. By-and-by, possibly, we may be able to extend the mission eastwards on the Congo, at a point above the rapids. But, however that may be, I hope that soon we shall have a steamer on the Congo.'

A steamer on the Congo! There could have been no mental picture more exciting to Alfred Henry Baynes as he read and reread the letter from Robert Arthington. Henry Baynes had been the Society's accountant during its move to new offices in Furnival Street off Holborn in 1870 and had moved into the Secretaryship, where he was to display great administrative ability, in 1876.

The letter that sent Alfred Baynes' pulses racing towards the end of 1877 was the first of many he was to receive from Robert Arthington. Always there were new ideas and suggestions and always more money, culminating in a legacy of £466,000 that was to make possible a hospital at San Salvador and a Bible Institute at Yakusu. As the churches caught the vision and the excitement, their giving also soared, so that the income of the BMS rocketed by fifty per cent from £40,000 in 1874 to £60,000 in 1883.

But it was that letter that started it all. On a sticky morning in the Cameroons on 5th January 1878, the irrepressibly happy-natured Tom Comber craned his neck to read over the shoulder of his friend George Grenfell the letter that had arrived for them from London. Would they be willing, Baynes wanted to know, to leave the Cameroons and proceed inland into Congo? Would they! Tom Comber threw his hat into the air with joy and excitement. And in no time the two young missionaries with two African teachers, an Angolan African as Portuguese interpreter, two Kru boys, three Cameroons boys, Jack their donkey and Jip their dog were on their way to meet King Don Pedro V at San Salvador in Portuguese Congo. There the one-time Birmingham schoolboy and the Camberwell lad carved their names on a huge baobab tree. But they were to make their mark on Congo in far deeper ways than that.

*

Alfred Saker looked round the gathering at the Cannon Street Hotel. What a world away it seemed from the Africa that still filled his waking thoughts and sprang even more vividly into steaming colour in his dreams. What a far cry from the land of witch-doctors, of fetishes, of poison smeared on doors, of tribalism and cannibalism, of dysentery and malaria, of crocodiles lurking in swamps and monkeys swinging through trees, to this English railway hotel, with the cabs waiting outside, and the eager young men with their frock-coats and watch-chains.

His eyes rested on Tom Comber, Tom who seemed to have everything. He was twenty-six years old, with the sort of personality that people warmed to at once. He had a purpose and joy in living born of unshakeable Christian conviction. He had just told the gathering of those interested in the Congo mission of the warmth of the welcome that he and George Grenfell had received from the King and people of San Salvador; how they had pressed them to say with them, so that work must surely be maintained there while at the same time the mission laid its plans for the hazardous 200-mile journey to Stanley Pool and the Congo river.

Tom also had the sparkle of a man in love. The journey to England to report on the success of the San Salvador expedition had given him the opportunity to see again his childhood sweetheart. Minnie Rickards was the daughter of Tom's former Sunday School teacher and now gentle, trusting Minnie was coming to Congo with him as his wife.

'The shadow' could hardly bear to look at the young man who exuded such excitement and hope. 'Would I were a young man again,' he thought, 'or had a second life to live, I would be off to Congo tomorrow.'

Alfred's eyes moved to the new recruits, quieter than Comber, for they had less to tell, but still clearly caught up in the fervour of a great purpose. There was Holman Bentley, who had been found for the Congo mission by W. R. Ricketts, later the BMS treasurer, Holman who in years to come was to do great translation work in Congo. There was the down-to-earth Irishman Crudgington, used to physical exertion, who had just finished his training at Rawdon College. There was John Hartland, who already knew Tom Comber for the two had shared children's work in the Camden Road Church, while Tom was at Regent's Park College.

It fell to Saker to speak. As founding father of the Cameroons mission, he was to give this new African venture his blessing. And his advice? It was never easy to advise others, especially the young on the threshold of a great adventure. But might he at least, into this highly-charged and hopeful atmosphere, introduce a note of warning? It was to prove a prophecy.

'While I congratulate you tonight, and the Committee also, in the establishment, so far, of this mission, I should like to utter just this word – that the enthusiasm of this hour will not suffice. We are but beginning a work which will test

our fidelity, our faith, our zeal, and it will test our hope also
. . . In the presence of the Master, and armed with his
power, your brethren, young as they are, may go forth in
confidence . . . But they may be called upon to suffer. We
know that they must labour, it may be long, long years
without much success, and in all the labour, in all the
sufferings, in all the toil of the future, in all the waiting, they
will want your sympathy, your prayers, your help; not the
sympathy of this hour alone, but the continuous sympathy
of your hearts . . . While they are down in that deep
dungeon, you cannot know the sorrow, the suffering, the
toil they may have. Keep hold of that rope, friends, on
which they depend.'

*

Hartland survived three years in Congo, Comber eight. But
Tom and Minnie had only four months of married life,
much of it on board ship, for Minnie died of meningitis
almost as soon as they set foot in Africa. Here was the first of
fifty deaths that were to wrap the first twenty-five years of
BMS work in Congo in a shroud of sacrifice and threaten to
turn the homeland cries of 'Africa for Christ' to 'Stop! The
cost is too high'.

For Congo demanded great physical and mental as well as
spiritual endurance. It was not until 1897 that the anopheles
mosquito was identified as the carrier of malaria, and in the
early years the missionaries struggled on through days of
raging fever. Seldom could an environment have been so
unwelcoming. Between San Salvador and Stanley Pool
where the river broadened into a sheet of water lay 200
miles of cataracts, so that the first priority was to find an
overland route through the territory of tribes who had but
one memory of the white man.

'In the sight of these poor people,' said Grenfell, showing

remarkable understanding of Africans who had shot
at Comber and Hartland as they tried to find a way
through their territory, 'we are brethren to those whose
dealings with them have been marked by such cruelty;
brethren to those who are at the bottom of all the
untold horrors of the slave trade. It is only by missionaries
living amongst these people, and proving to them what
manner of men they are, that these suspicions will be
overcome and a way be opened to their hearts and
confidences.'

In the end, after twelve attempts, it was Crudgington
and Bentley who, having followed Stanley's route on the
north bank of the river for forty-five miles, struck out
on a new path and in February 1882 reached Stanley Pool,
the first Europeans to complete the journey from the
coast. Land at the Pool was granted to them by the
International Association, forerunner of the Congo Free
State government. The mission station that Comber built
there, virtually with his bare hands, carrying timber five
miles and grass three, while Bentley went back to the coast
for workmen, was called 'Arthington'.

But at home Robert Arthington had already moved on
to the next stage of his plans. He knew that above Stanley
Pool the Congo river was navigable – but only by a special
type of boat. A mile wide in places, the river was also
very shallow, treacherous with sandbanks and half-sub-
merged islands. Robert Arthington offered the BMS £1000
towards the cost of a purpose-built steamer and a further
£3000 for its maintenance on the Congo river.

*

The SS *Peace* was built at Thorneycroft's yard at
Chiswick. Grenfell, called home to watch the building,
saw in his mind's eye the gruelling 200 miles to Stanley

Pool over which the dismantled boat would have to be carried in manageable loads.

A string of staging posts, constructed by nailing the stems of palmtree fronds in horizontal rows on to posts fixed in the ground, roofed with grass, had been established as resting places and as stores for the cotton, knives and beads used as barter with the Africans. Ninety miles from San Salvador to Musaka. Seventy miles to Isangila. Then the seventy-five miles to Manyanga by water because the tribes in that area were so hostile as to make the river seem comparatively welcoming. Grenfell watched every rivet go into the boat, knowing that at Stanley Pool it would have to be reconstructed by engineers. With him was Doke, a student at Regent's who was to help with the reconstruction. Grenfell took to his new colleague; he looked forward to working with him in Congo.

The completed *Peace* was floated on the Thames at Westminster, a tangible focus for the enthusiasm running high in the churches who had raised the cost of travel for six new missionaries within weeks of a stirring visit home by Crudgington. The *Peace* was seventy feet long; even with a four-ton load of firewood and stores, she had a draught of only twelve inches. She was capable of doing twelve miles per hour.

Grenfell and Doke watched as she was dismantled. Every one of the 800 packages was sewn up in canvas and numbered so that replacements could be sent from England if any were lost. By December 1882, with their hopes running high, it was time for Grenfell and Doke to set off to Africa with her.

But the hopes were to be shattered. The missionaries landed in mid-January and by February Doke, the new friend with whom Grenfell had planned so much, was dead of fever. Two months later Hartland died. Grenfell pressed on to Stanley Pool with his family, while a team of 400 carriers, paid in red calico and white-handled knives, patiently bore the boat, manhandling it across ravines with ropes and pulleys. The boat, amazingly, survived, but blow after blow was falling on the missionary team. Grenfell's arrival at Stanley Pool and reunion with Comber was marked not by triumph but by unspeakable sorrow. 'It was a sad welcome that awaited me at the Pool,' Grenfell was to write home. 'Terrible tidings of death and illness had just arrived, and as Comber went out to have the flag hoisted at half-mast, he spied my boat in the distance just rounding Kallina Point, so, not wishing to distress me with the dismal signal, he ran the flag right up. By the time I had reached the landing place, he was there to meet me, and gradually unfolded such a list of evil tidings as never fell upon my poor head in so short a time before . . . Crudgington and his wife both seriously sick, making the possibility of their return to England a contingency to be provided for by one of the new men being stationed with him instead of coming up country; Hughes just recovering from a serious illness at Bayneston; Ross so sick at Manyanga that Comber had to start off immediately to send him home, if it were not already too late; Quentin Thomas dead at Victoria; the two engineers sent out for the *Peace* both dead, and the new missionary Hartley dead also.'

So there were to be no English engineers to reconstruct the *Peace*. Comber was forced to assume responsibility for the whole of the work in the Lower River region. With his brother Sidney, newly arrived from England and to survive only two years, he crossed the river to Ngombe-Lutete and established the station of Wathen-Ngombe. Wathen named after a beneficiary who gave money for a school there, was to become the focus for the work in the Lower River and for the Kikongo translation work of Holman Bentley. The Wathen Church was formed on New Year's Day 1889, a year after the formation of the first Baptist church at San

Salvador, and Sidney, a doctor, began a much-needed medical mission tragically cut short by his death.

Grenfell, left alone at Stanley Pool, surveyed the 800 packages of steamship. Then he called his African boys together for prayer. He and they, together with a carpenter and a blacksmith from the West Coast, were going to have to rebuild her themselves. In May the keel was laid. Just twelve weeks later, the boat had, as Grenfell put it, been 'prayed together'. As steam rose from her funnel, and as the *Peace* inched forward on the river on which she was to travel thousands of miles, the boys cried together 'She lives, master! She lives!'

She did indeed live, and Grenfell, like his boat, was raring to go. Within days, with eight African lads aboard, he set out on a 1200-mile voyage of exploration, from which he returned convinced that the next two stations should be in the densely populated area of Bolobo and at Lukolela. There would, he knew, be communication problems to overcome, for the tribes spoke a different language from those of the Lower River. Grenfell's 'cubs' as he called them loved that trip – carrying firewood and working in the stoke-hole for a good head of steam – swarming over the boat and falling in the river – swimming with a fine disregard for the crocodiles – grinning back at the surprised faces of their fellow Africans on the bank.

The missionaries had what we would today consider a 'paternalistic' relationship with their 'boys'. They gave them an English name to go with their African one and incongruous English clothes. They took them to England on furlough. They expected, and received, respect and allegiance bordering on personal devotion. But they gave them, too, their first chance of education and, in place of a fear of evil spirits and a reliance on fetishism, their first introduction to a Saviour. In March 1886, the first baptism in Congo was of Mantu Parkinson, the boy who had given his heart first to Thomas Comber but then to Jesus Christ. The following year Comber died. His parents had lost two sons and a daughter in the service of Christ in the African missions.

*

Grenfell was at heart as much explorer as missionary. His travels up the Congo and its numerous and extensive tributaries, charting 3400 miles of waterway in two years, earned him the Gold Medal of the Royal Geographical Society. It also earned him criticism from some at home. As with Saker, so with Grenfell, and so with many missionaries since, there was divergence of opinion as to what 'preaching the Gospel' should entail. It was hard for those at the time to apprehend the service rendered not just to the BMS but to other missionary societies by Grenfell's charting of hitherto unexplored regions. It was hard too for English church members in the order and safety of their own lives to begin to imagine the courage the explorations required. Holman Bentley was stung by the criticism.

'It has pained us much,' he said, 'that our purpose in these investigations has, in some quarters, been misunderstood. It may be exciting, but it is certainly far from pleasant, to be a target for poisoned arrows, or to run the frequent risk of being speared, and perhaps eaten by wild cannibals. The accounts may be thrilling, but whatever aspects the work may present to those who think the matter over beside their comfortable fireside at home, certainly those of us who have been obliged to do pioneering work, almost *ad nauseam*, would infinitely prefer quiet mission work on our stations to the privations and exposure which must inevitably attend all such journeys into the unknown interior.'

Yes, it was hard for those in the pews of their Victorian chapels, often with sentimentalized images of what it was to take the Gospel to benighted heathen, to apprehend the reality. The missionaries even had to censor the photographs they sent to England. A letter accompanying photographs sent to Alfred Baynes conceded: 'No. 5, the Dancing Group, will hardly do for the pages of the *Missionary Herald*. I suppose it would be too shocking, and yet it is respectability and decency itself compared with the reality of the greater part of our surroundings.'

The opening of the Lower Congo Railway, from Matadi to Stanley Pool in 1898 ended the often literally killing journey overland from the station at Underhill to the Pool. But for many years the *Peace* and her successors, *Goodwill* and *Endeavour*, given by Christian Endeavour groups not only in England but in Congo itself, were vital for the establishment and servicing of the up-river stations. Mission stations with chapel and school were set up at Bolobo in 1888, at Upoto and Monsembe in 1890 (the Monsembe station was abandoned after fifteen years) and at Yakusu, no less than 1350 miles from the coast, in 1896. By the end of 1898, with thirty-one missionaries on the field, there were 328 church members, of whom ninety-four had been baptized that year.

Bolobo saw the formation of the first church on the Upper River, in a building 22 feet square with walls of rendered brick. The station became home to the *Peace* and a centre for teaching engineering skills to Africans. It was also home to the Hannah Wade printing press, worked by Albert Scrivener and producing New Testaments, hymn-books and other literature for the new Christians and for the African evangelists being trained to work in the villages. By 1893, Bentley's Kikongo New Testament, together with Kikongo grammar and dictionary, were in use in the San Salvador area, now Angola, and in Lower Congo. Above Stanley Pool, however, the question of translation was even more difficult for the tribes spoke a dozen or so languages, including Bobangi, Lingombe, Lokele and Heso. The decisions as to which languages should be the focus for translation work were compounded by the ongoing problems facing all missionary translators in finding words to convey Christian doctrine.

'I can find no word for "forgiveness",' Grenfell agonized, 'and it has to be rendered by "cleansing". "Sanctification" I have not ventured to grapple with yet.' But there were other problems looming.

*

'Christendom is responsible for the greatest hindrance to Christian work in heathendom. It is so in every part of the world. Sometimes the officials of a nominally Christian government, at other times traders from a so-called Christian country, plus occasionally individual travellers, explorers and adventurers, so misrepresent the religion of their native land, as utterly to discredit the religion which they profess. Who can tell the amount and strength of the prejudice against Christianity which the conduct of the English called into existence in the worst days of the East India Company? The Opium Wars in China are responsible for no little hostility among the Chinese to the religion of the British, while the lust for territory yet more recently displayed by European powers is unquestionably the cause of distress and dislike and of disinclination to receive from foreigners a strange religion. I fear Africa has real reason to turn a deaf ear to the message of the missionary.'

Those words, written by Charles Williams in the *Missionary Herald* of February 1904, sum up one of the recurring heartaches of missionary work. Certainly they summed up the situation in Africa at the time.

The early years of Baptist work in Congo had been favoured by the Belgians and by King Leopold with a

benign interest. So benign that Grenfell wore Belgian
medals on his chest and was used as an intermediary in a
territorial dispute with the Portuguese. Only once had the
relationship been strained, when the *Peace* was com-
mandeered by the Belgian authorities to transport soldiers
and ammunition up the Kasai. A maxim gun was mounted
with its nozzle jutting out over the letters *PEACE*!
Representations by Alfred Baynes to Brussels, and a firm
stand by the Congo Secretary, Lawson Forfeitt, however,
had resulted in assurances that nothing so contrary to the
principles of the mission should ever happen again. In many
ways, good came out of the event, for it spelt out the need
for the *Goodwill* in addition to the *Peace*.

In 1901, however, life in the Congo Free State,
technically a sovereign state established by the Berlin Act,
to which Britain as well as Belgium was a signatory,
changed for the worse. Edicts created a state monopoly in
rubber and ivory over a huge area north of the Congo river.
All land outside of the villages, it was claimed, belonged not
to the African tribes of the area but to the state. The natives
were to pay a 'tax' in rubber, to the commercial value of
which their eyes had only recently been opened.

The gathering of the 'tax' amounted in many areas to
slave labour, with Africans forced into the forest to produce
the rubber and cruelly abused by government soldiers.
Although the areas from which atrocities began to be
reported were in general away from mission stations, they
included the Upper River stations at Upoto and at
Monsembe, where Stapleton was the missionary. Before
long allegations of maiming and of murder lay heavily on
his heart.

'It is becoming a grave question with me and with
others,' he said, 'how long we can reconcile silence on the
question of the infamous wrongs to which these people are
subject with our conscientious view of our duty towards

them as missionaries.' How William Knibb would have understood his feelings!

Later, indeed, the missionaries were to be criticized for their apparent early silence. But, if silent they were at first, there were reasons. Grenfell was initially inclined to assign reports of abuse to maladministration rather than evil intent; only later were his eyes opened and his respect for King Leopold destroyed. The committee in London urged caution on the missionaries, pointing out that to damage their relationship with the government might prejudice their freedom to work. 'Leave it to me,' said Baynes, who had previously found personal representations to the Belgians to be effective. This time, however, his letters were ignored.

So it fell to an American, E. D. Morel, to reveal the horror of what by 1903 was happening in Congo. Roger Casement, the British Consul, requested by his government to investigate the truth of Morel's assertions, uncovered atrocities that could no longer be explained away or ignored. By now, too, evidence was coming in thick and fast from appalled members of the mission staff.

*

Albert Scrivener stood in what had until recently been a densely populated area near Lake Leopold in the *domaine privée* of the King. Now it was desolate and at his feet were human bones, skulls and complete skeletons. He turned to his guide for explanation.

'When the Bambate were sent to make us cut rubber, there were so many killed that we got tired of burying. Sometimes, when we wanted to bury, we were not allowed to.'

'Why,' Scrivener asked with a sinking heart, 'did they kill so many?'

'Oh, sometimes we were ordered to go and then the sentry would find us preparing food to eat while in the forest. They would shoot two or three to hurry us along. Sometimes we would try to do a little work on our plantations, so that when harvest time came, we should have something to eat. Then the sentry would shoot some of us to teach us that our business was not to plant but to cut rubber.'

Now that the man had begun to speak, he seemed unable to stop the catalogue of misery.

'Sometimes we were driven off to live for a fortnight in the forest without any food and many died of cold and hunger. Sometimes the quantity brought was not enough and then several would be killed to frighten us to bring more.'

Scrivener turned away, ashamed of his white skin. It was one of the saddest journeys he had ever made in Congo, and his sorrow was compounded on the way home. With him on the trip was Nkosi, an African evangelist, invaluable because he spoke four languages other than his own. Scrivener watched helplessly as Nkosi's canoe overturned and his young Christian friend drowned. Back at the mission station, all he could do was to pour out his anger and sorrow in a letter to Alfred Baynes, intended also for publication in the *Missionary Herald*.

Other missionaries had their own stories to add to the accumulating evidence. W. R. Kirby, in the area of Yalemba, the latest of the Upper River stations, found people packed suffocating into prisons. He found, too, the futility of trying to preach 'the white man's religion' in such a situation. 'There are over a hundred persons in prison and they have been taken from all the villages round about. They will be kept until their friends bring in the proper amount of rubber for the tax. I heard about a white man called "The Chief of the Prisons". I had started with the intention of preaching the Gospel to the people I met, but they did not want it. "Take this white man from us first," they said, "and then you can tell us the good news."'

While Belgium tried to wash her hands of responsibility for 'a sovereign state', E. D. Morel continued his attacks on those who were pillaging the Africans' land for their own ends and inciting the Africans to tribal warfare in their desperate search for rubber to satisfy their masters. The Baptist Missionary Society, now with C. E. Wilson as its Secretary, became a vigorous supporter of the Congo Reform Association. In 1908, the Belgian government annexed the Congo Free State and slowly reforms began. Relations between the state and the missionaries could now improve. It had, however, been an object lesson in the tensions to which missionaries were subject, the tension between their loyalty and love for the men and women they had come to serve and the need to maintain a working relationship with a host government.

*

In 1908, on the Upper River, Kirby was uncovering the hell-hole of a prison, but at Kimpese on the Lower River the first students were preparing to build their own houses at the United Evangelical Training Institute. The BMS did not work in isolation from those who shared its aims. The printing press at Bolobo produced material for other societies. Conferences of missionary personnel working in Lower Congo had long been aware of the need for further training of African evangelists and teachers. Might it be done together? The answer from the British Baptists, American Baptists and Swedish Missionary Society was 'Yes.'

Already attitudes were becoming rather less 'paternal-istic' than in the pioneering years. The first English staff of the college, the Lewises, and their American counterparts, the Moons, were not out to create 'an imitation white man' for the pulpit or the school. So, while the Lewises and the Moons prepared courses in Old and New Testament studies, in mathematics, elementary science and geography, the students were left to plan their own housing, food and clothing according to their own culture. Alongside the classroom, a carpenter's, blacksmith's and bricklayer's workshop went up, for the Christian workers being trained to meet the needs of Angola and the Lower Congo would need to be able to build chapels and schools.

'It is of the utmost importance', said Mrs Lewis, 'that teachers' wives should be able to read.' Of the first fourteen women students at the college, only five could read, write or sew when they arrived. Before long their classes included Old and New Testament, natural history of the trees and flowers that surrounded the college, hygiene and physiology to help with basic health care, and Christian lifestyle, for much in the way of example would be required from these young women.

1908. And at last, at long last, there were two medical missionaries in Congo. Never had a mission field been so desperate in its need for a doctor. Dr Sidney Comber had been able to give just one year to the medical mission he set up at Wathen; Dr Sidney Webb, who followed him there, had died in 1895, two years after Dr Comber. Then for a decade there had been no doctor to care for the needs of the mission staff themselves – thirty-nine at eleven stations – let alone for the Africans.

Each mission station had a dispensary and the staff used what medical skills they had gleaned to help those who came to their door. As people abandoned reliance on fetishes, it was imperative that they were offered medical help in their stead. The missionaries' wives and the single women who were just beginning to be accepted as missionaries in their own right had had some basic training in obstetrics. But how many mothers and babies they would have been able to save, had they been able to call on a doctor!

The fame of Miss Lilian de Hailes and her nursing skills spread far beyond her dispensary at Bolobo and for years Africans – 26,000 of them a year – came from miles around, sleeping in their canoes while receiving out-patient treatment from her loving hands. A hospital building was erected at Wathen in 1906, but it was a hospital without a doctor. From San Salvador the King appealed desperately for a doctor to study sleeping sickness, the strange disease that produced lethargy and then death in people all along the Congo river where the tsetse fly had its haunts.

If ever a mission field was to prove the value of medical missionaries, it would be Congo. But, in the struggle that had culminated in the formation of the Medical Missionary Auxiliary of the BMS in 1902, that value had had to be asserted forcefully. The few missionaries with medical qualifications who had worked for the BMS prior to 1900 had been all too aware of the constraints on them. Their evangelical zeal was of more concern to the Society than their medical expertise. Although they might give medical care to their colleagues and could hardly refuse it to others who came for help, not too much time was to be taken away from the primary task of preaching. Such medical work as they were able to do was accomplished with very limited resources. Hospital building had no place in the Society's evangelistic plans.

In 1901, Dr Ellen Farrer and Dr Vincent Thomas, missionaries in India, and Dr Paterson of Shantung in China, had begun to press for an appraisal of BMS medical policy. The formation of the MMA, encouraged by Christian doctors in England such as Sir Alfred Pearce Gould and Dr Percy Lush, added weight to their voices. At

last the work of the nurse and the doctor – and later of the
pharmacist and medical technician – began to be seen not as
a way in to the preaching of the Gospel but as integral to the
Gospel itself as the healing ministry of Jesus had been to his
life. To be worthy of that Gospel, Dr Fletcher Moorshead,
Secretary of the MMA, argued, the medical care provided
had to be of as high a standard as possible. Suddenly,
staffing, training, buildings and equipment were no longer
spiritually insignificant but vital.

So at last in 1907 two medical missionaries were
appointed for Congo. Dr Mercier Gamble was to go to San
Salvador, where he would be the only doctor in the whole
of Portuguese Congo. Dr E. C. Girling was to go to Upper
Congo.

There was no shortage of volunteers to put up pre-
fabricated hospitals at San Salvador and at Bolobo. By 1912,
the hospitals were up and running and a new era of work in
Congo was about to begin. Two years later it was
interrupted by war.

5. Cultural Conflict

China 1860 to 1922

'Lord, send me to that part of the world where the difficulties are greatest.' That was the prayer, not of a Baptist missionary but of Robert Morrison, a young worker with the London Missionary Society at the start of the nineteenth century. God answered his prayer by sending him to China.

So were the difficulties facing missionaries to China in the 1900s 'greater' than those posed by the caste system of Hinduism, the social injustice of the West Indies, the fetishism of hostile tribes on the west coast of Africa or the tumbling cataracts of the Congo river? Undoubtedly the difficulties were different. Certainly Morrison had offered his prayer and his life – and had spent nearly thirty years off the coast of China, translating the Scriptures but with hardly a convert to show for it.

Over the centuries China had developed a mistrust, bordering on hatred, of foreigners. Her ports were closed to them. Trade and mission were confined to a narrow strip of land near Canton and to Macao, a Portuguese colony. She already had impressive natural boundaries in the form of desert and mountain to the north and west. And she had her Great Wall, 1500 miles long as the crow flies, sixteen feet high, nineteen feet wide, punctuated with thousands of watch-towers.

Despite the Wall, China had not always had an antipathy to people of other nations and cultures. Through four dynasties, spanning a thousand years, she had allowed communities of Jews and Muslims to settle within her borders. Buddhist monks had come to establish their religion alongside the Confucianism and Taoism of China. There was trade with Japan. A stone tablet at Sianfu in Shensi province in northern China commemorated the work of Nestorian missionaries in the eighth century. Eight centuries after that, a Jesuit, Matteo Ricci had been allowed to settle in Peking. He and his fellow priests had established Roman Catholic communities in China. They were tolerated so long as they kept up a dialogue with Confucianism but finally ejected when they claimed exclusive truth.

Yet by the nineteenth century the Chinese word officially used for 'foreigner' meant 'barbarian'. The Chinese had had to face Mongol incursions from the north and Japanese piracy from the coast. Now the Western powers, Portugal, Spain, the Netherlands and Britain, aware of the great trading potential of this vast nation and of its untapped mineral wealth, a peared to the Chinese intent in dividing up their land as they were carving up Africa. The decadent behaviour of many traders, away from the constraints of home, did nothing to endear them to a community that had become increasingly reluctant hosts.

To add to the hatred of the foreigner and his religious faith had come in 1850 the T'ai Ping rebellion. The Hakka tribe threw up a self-styled 'little brother of Jesus' with half-baked ideas of Christianity compounded by a hatred of the Manchu emperors. Fourteen years of rebellion claimed twenty million lives and added to the mistrust of Christianity, now proscribed. Small wonder that the Chinese now wanted no truck nor trade with foreigners. What, after all, did they have to learn from them? China had her own ancient civilization and culture and her own great philosophies and religions. The Chinese had invented the compass. They had practised vaccination against disease before it was used in the West. They produced exquisite porcelain and silk.

China was an agricultural society, in which man's relationship to the natural world was of supreme importance. Her philosophies aimed at harmonious relationships between human beings, earth and heaven, and, within society, between ruler and subject, male and female, father and son. Confucianism, the dominant philosophy of the ruling classes, was concerned with how such harmonious relationships could be achieved in society. Taoism was also about 'the way', but through a mystical experience of nature. Other Chinese followed the quietistic branch of Buddhism called 'The Great Wagon'. Why should the Chinese want Robert Morrison, confined to his island off the coast? Why should they want Marshman's translation of the Bible into Chinese, completed in 1823?

So there were great and distinctive problems in the path of Christian mission to China in the nineteenth century. The harsh truth is that in the end it was war, the Opium Wars of the 1840s and 1850s, that finally forced open the Chinese ports not only to trade but to missionaries with the Gospel.

By 1836, opium was the world's most valuable single commodity. It was extensively grown in China, using land that could have been put to better use in a country frequently devastated by famine, but Indian opium was also imported by British traders. Ten per cent of the Chinese population smoked opium and there were fifteen million addicts, pale, thin, debilitated, open to moral exploitation. The Chinese government, anxious to end the import of opium and to resist other trade as well, was twice humiliated in war against Britain and France. In the Treaty of Tientsin in 1860, China was forced to open many of her ports, allow foreigners into the hinterland, permit the teaching of Christianity throughout her empire and offer protection to missionaries.

The Chinese had opened their ports and cities rather than

their hearts and minds, but it was all that the Western missionary societies were waiting for. Within fifty years, there were to be sixty-three separate Protestant missionary societies working in China, agreeing a 'comity' arrangement over blocks of territory, as well as the non-denominational China Inland Mission founded by Hudson Taylor. Where, in all this, was the Baptist Missionary Society?

*

In the bitter cold of January 1875, a Welshman called Timothy Richard set out in a blizzard to travel from Chefoo on the Chinese coast to the city of Ching-chou-fu 250 miles inland. He had various reasons for leaving Chefoo behind him. His three predecessors as Baptist missionaries there, Kloekers, Hall and Laughton, had all swiftly been removed by disease. Then Timothy had lost his friend, Dr William Brown. For a while the two men had shared tours of preaching and healing, riding together in a shen-tzu, a chair slung between two mules. But in the period prior to the establishment of the Medical Missionary Auxiliary, William Brown, like other doctors before him, had quarrelled with the Home Comittee over the priorities and methods of his medical work.

Chefoo was a lonely place without him. In any case a trading port, full of foreigners intent on their own ends, was hardly a propitious area for the spread of the Gospel. Surely Ching-chou-fu, one of the most important walled cities in the province of Shantung, with a population of 30,000, would offer more scope and more hope. So the young man from Carmarthenshire reasoned, as the cruel wind of the North China winter removed the last trace of feeling from his fingers and toes.

After the blizzard, even a Chinese inn – a courtyard with

huts of sun-dried brick, a wooden frame for the traveller's bedding – was a relief. The inn was to be Timothy Richard's home for some time, for lodging there seemed less aggressive and incursive into the local community than setting up his own household. Shantung was the birthplace of Confucius; Ching-chou-fu was also an important Muslim centre. But at least the inn was a base from which Timothy could offer his simple medical treatments, with the two drugs he possessed, chloridine and quinine. It was also a base from which he could begin his conversations with those who appeared to be 'worthy'.

At the valedictory service five years previously, at which Timothy had been wished 'God speed' by his friends and by the Society, he had been urged to study the instructions of Jesus to his apostles. One of them came repeatedly into his mind: 'In whatsoever city or town ye shall enter, inquire in it who is worthy; and there abide till ye go thence.' It was a text that was bound to speak to a man of Timothy's open mind and broad sympathies. The Chinese might not be Christian but he was not prepared to see them as 'benighted heathens'. The way forward, he was sure, was to seek out the 'worthy', men of integrity of whatever religion or philosophy, appeal to their understanding and use their influence.

At the mosque and at the Muslim theological college, Timothy Richard sought out the mullahs and the professors. The experience was to open his eyes as much as theirs.

'I realized,' he conceded, 'that the evidence with which I was then prepared to advocate Christianity would be useless to bring forward with Mohammedans. For every prophecy I could quote they could match with a similar one of their own, and for every miracle I could mention they could produce a hundred.'

The Baptist missionary found himself driven to a more

careful study of Islam. At the same time he was poring over the Chinese classics. Chinese, with its 214 'radicals' which formed the index to the thousands of Chinese characters, was a daunting course of study. But Timothy was building up a vocabulary of religious terms significant to the Chinese people. In his dialogue with Chinese scholars, he appealed to their shared ground of common truth in a way that was later to horrify and cause a rift with more fundamentalist colleagues.

Perhaps it was as well that there was no fundamentalist missionary colleague around to pass judgement on the circumstances of the first baptism in Ching-chou-fu, that of a silk weaver and his wife. They had first committed to memory and then taken to heart the Christian catechism prepared by Timothy Richard. Baptism in the river outside the west gate of the city – fine. But to use the Buddhist temple on the river bank as a changing room? Not everyone would have understood Timothy's resolution to meet the local community and culture partway.

But when a colleague, Alfred Jones, an Irish business-man, did arrive in March 1877, there was no dissension over methods of work between the two men. Instead they shared a desperate determination to respond to the horror unfolding around them.

China, with her vast population, has always been subject to famine, caused generally by flood in the south and drought in the north. In each of the years 1876–78, the crops failed in the northern provinces. Appalling hunger and misery triggered off the breakdown of law and order. Soaring food prices led to robbery, then murder; desperately people sold homes, then wives and children. The local Chinese people, watching Timothy Richard's response, realized that it took a brave man to organize famine relief from the international community in Shanghai and to distribute it to crowds likely to riot.

For some the question was finally inescapable: what was the faith that lay behind this compassion?

By the winter of 1877, there had been over 300 baptisms. Timothy Richard, Jones and the Chinese Pastor Ch'ing were busy with a thousand people who wanted to know more about the Christian faith. They organized new Christians into groups with local leaders, often barely literate, distributing catechisms, hymns and sermons to them and calling them into Ching-chou-fu from the villages for training when they could. It was the beginning of the idea that the Chinese Church was going to have to be itself and help itself – a concept that, within a few decades, would prove crucial in the survival of the church.

Now was surely not a good time for Timothy Richard to leave Shantung. Yet desperate appeals were reaching him from the International Famine Relief Committee in Shanghai. For, if the famine in Shantung was bad, it was worse, far worse, in Shansi.

Shansi province – the name means 'West of the hills' – was bordered in the east by mountains and in the south and west by the Yellow River. Its soil was broken into rifts fifty to one hundred feet deep. Transportation was almost impossible – and the nearest stocks of food were 800 miles away at Tientsin.

It was November, winter again, when Timothy Richard set out in bitter cold, first by cart and then over the mountains on muleback. As he neared the city of Tai-iuan-fu, believing that he already knew what famine could do to people, he saw what he had yet to learn. Bodies torn by dogs and wolves littered the roadside. Cartloads of women were being taken away for sale. The trees had been stripped of their bark for food. People were resorting to murder and cannibalism. In his first letter to *The Times*, reporting five million already dead in Shansi, Timothy spared English readers none of the details.

For the next twenty months Timothy Richard worked alongside the Methodist David Hill and Joshua Turner of the CIM. £60,000 worth of famine relief, much of it from a Mansion House fund set up by the Lord Mayor of London, was administered to 150,000 people. The experience convinced him of what was desperately needed by the people of northern China. They needed railways for transportation; they needed to exploit their mineral deposits; they needed to stop growing opium and start growing food with more effective methods; they needed education. Timothy Richard pounded away at the 'worthy'. He gave lectures with magic lantern slides. He set up a dynamo to demonstrate the powers of electricity – 'God's miracles'.

And the people of northern China needed the Gospel. Timothy Richard and the first Chinese evangelists adopted the methods of the public story-teller, taking a room open on to the main street, serving tea, talking to the crowds who came to hear the skillful telling of the story and drawing one or two into deeper conversation. In 1878 the first Baptist church in Shansi was formed; the Home Committee, poised on the brink of mission in Congo, found the money for five more missionaries for Shansi. They were to join Timothy and his new wife, Mary, who was busy running orphanages for emaciated children and teaching them skills that would enable them to earn a living.

But the population of northern China was on the move. The government was offering free land to those who would make the trek from overcrowded Shantung to Shensi province, depopulated in the aftermath of the T'ai Ping rebellion and by famine, and ravaged by wolves. So the people came, nearly 40,000 of them, 800 miles on foot, reluctantly leaving the graves of their ancestors, belongings piled into wheelbarrows.

Among those who made and survived the journey – for

many died on the way – were forty members of the fast-growing Baptist community from Shantung and their families, with four pastors and teachers. They settled in Fu-Yin-T'sun, 'Gospel Village'. Living apart, they would not have to pay temple or theatre tax or join in worship with others. A bye-law of their village forbade the growing of opium. The little group of Christians had their pastor, Sun-Han-Ch'ing, trained at the training school at Ching-chou-fu that was later to become the Gotch-Robinson Institute. The Chinese Church was to be self-financing, self-governing and self-propagating. But not completely, just yet. A deputation sent by the BMS, T. M. Morris and Richard Glover, Chairman of the China Sub-Committee, reported on the request of the Shensi Christians for missionary staff to help them. So the Rev. A. G. Shorrock, the Rev. and Mrs Moir Duncan and the Rev. and Mrs Evan Morgan came from Shansi to help the settlers. Fifteen years after Timothy Richard had arrived in Ching-chou-fu, BMS work was established in the three provinces where it was to continue for half a century of turbulence and tears.

*

Two miles outside the city of Tai-yuan-fu in Shansi, and outside the west gate of the city of Hsin-chou in the same province are the graves of Baptist missionaries and of the Chinese Christians who chose to die with them in 1900. The entire BMS staff in the province, thirteen men and women with three children, were put to death in a bitter surge of hatred against the foreigner that claimed the lives of 159 Protestant missionaries and twelve Roman Catholic priests in Shansi, 380 Chinese members of the Protestant churches and, since the Roman Catholic churches had been estab-lished much longer, over 2,000 Roman Catholics.

The struggle between those pressing for reform in China

and reactionaries determined to cling to the old ways had been inevitable. The missionaries who were bringing education, opening schools, training pastors, convincing some Chinese officials of the need for western-style education and reform, had unwittingly and from the best of motives contributed to the storm that now broke around them.

Meanwhile the flames of outrage in those who hated the foreigner had been fanned. France had annexed Cambodia and Vietnam; Britain had annexed Burma. Japan declared war on China and won effective control of Korea, and in the wake of that event there was a scramble by the western powers to gain concessions in China.

Such was the legacy of bitterness. When the young Emperor came down on the side of those advocating a rapid programme of reform within China, the Dowager Empress moved against him. China abounded in secret societies. It was to one of them, nicknamed 'The Boxers' by the foreign community because of the shadow-boxing of their occult rites, that the Dowager Empress turned for help.

No matter that Boxer hatred was traditionally directed against the Manchu emperors themselves as well as against the foreigner. The Empress Dowager realized she could use them for her own ends. When on 21st June 1900 she issued edicts ordering the death of all foreigners, the Boxers were ready to move.

The Dowager had reckoned, however, without the courage and integrity of many Chinese officials. As the homes of Chinese Christians blazed in Shantung, and the governor there urged Chinese Christians to 'recant for the time being', he allowed the missionary staff to escape to the coast. Governor Tuan-Fang in Shensi showed even greater courage, evacuating the missionaries and protecting Chinese Christians. But in Shansi the missionaries were up against the implacable hatred of the Governor, Yu-Hsien.

On his orders and in his presence the missionaries in Tai-yuan-fu were brutally murdered on 9th July 1900. The missionaries in Hein-chou were beaten to death one month later.

Many Chinese Christians died for refusing to recant their new faith or to reveal the identity of their fellow believers. They died as courageously as those who had brought them the good news that they could not now deny.

By the time foreign troops forced their way through to Peking, beseiged by the Boxers, in August 1900, the Christian Church in Shansi had been laid waste. But the process of enlightenment and reform within China could not now be stopped, even though it carried within it the seeds of the next crisis for the nation and for the church.

*

Jennie Beckingsale, BSc, BA, was the antidote to any idea of the unmarried woman missionary, equipped with a Bible, good intentions and not much else. She had been educated at Cheltenham College and then at Somerville, Oxford, where she had read mathematics and science. She held degrees from the universities of London and Dublin – no small achievement for a woman at the turn of the century. In another age, she might have been working alongside the male staff at one of the universities associated with Christian mission in China, perhaps at the Shantung Christian University, with its faculties of arts, science, theology and medicine, established in 1904 as a joint venture by the BMS and the American Presbyterian (North) Mission.

The University at Tai-yuan-fu had been the result of even broader and more imaginative vision – and of a forgiving spirit. After the massacres of 1900, Timothy Richard, working with the Christian Literature Society for China, had been called in by the Governor of Shansi to discuss reparation to the church by the province. The BMS did not seek financial redress. Timothy Richard's opinion was that the popular support that the Boxers had been able to arouse stemmed directly from ignorance. Everything he had seen in his time in China had convinced him that education must go hand-in-hand with the proclamation of the Gospel. He suggested, therefore, that appropriate reparation could take the form of a university at Tai-yuan-fu.

So, out of the tragedy of 1900, had come a modern university. It was traditionally Chinese in architecture, but lit throughout by electricity, the equipment for which had been carried on muleback from Tientsin. The university had separate Chinese and Western departments. The Western faculties offered not only law, languages, mathematics and science but mining and civil engineering – quite a challenge for the Chinese interpreters. The Shansi officials had been adamant that Christianity was not to form part of the curriculum, but Timothy Richard, as Chancellor, appointed as the first Principal the Rev. Moir Duncan. Duncan had gained his experience as a missionary in Shensi and his academic qualifications in Chinese at Oxford. How could Moir Duncan, lecturing on civilization, fail to refer to the principles and outworkings of Christian faith? How could the Methodist, Dr Soothill, tutor in history and later Moir Duncan's successor, fail to take similar opportunities?

So, yes, in another age, perhaps Jennie Beckingsale would have been in the lecture rooms of Shantung or Tai-yuan-fu. But the education of women and girls in China was far from reaching university level. And it was to the work of the Baptist Zenana Mission, set up in 1867 to work amongst the women of India but now also in China, in close partnership with the BMS, that Jennie had offered her undoubted abilities.

It angered her that the girls who came to the school in the

eastern suburb of the city of Hsi-an-fu, where she taught with her colleagues, Miss Russell and Miss Turner, could barely walk, let alone run as Jennie remembered running with her friends on the playing fields of Cheltenham. Their parents were now choosing Christian education for their daughters – the Baptist Church in Shensi had grown rapidly from 541 in 1903 to over 1,000 in 1911 – but nothing could undo the crippling work of the footbinder. As little girls, destined to be nothing more than a delicate presence in a male-dominated home, their feet had been cruelly bound, toes crushed and bleeding, so that they hobbled. Women missionaries were now busy campaigning against the practice in the Anti-Footbinding Society. Meanwhile Jennie was determined that the minds of the girls were not to be as fettered and stunted as their poor little feet.

As the brief period of twilight gave way to darkness in October 1911, Jennie prayed both for the girls in her school and for her fellow missionaries. She knew that the church in Shantung, always more firmly established than in the other provinces, was growing. Requests for tent missions were pouring in from village churches. The preaching halls were busy. Colporteurs toured the markets and fairs. The Gotch-Robertson Institute at Ching-chou-fu was training pastors for new churches. But Jennie's heart ached for her colleagues at Shansi. It had taken a lot of courage to try to rebuild the work there. At the mention of Jesus, the response was predictable: 'Do you want us to believe in a God who couldn't protect his people in 1900?'

Now again, it seemed as if China was in turmoil. The Western ideas that the missionaries had brought with them had gained ground as students took new opportunities for education in France, Germany and the USA. Sun-Yat-Sen, leader of the newly formed Chinese National Party, had been educated in Honolulu, where he had become a Christian. Young people who went to Japan for education came back fired with nationalist sentiments, stirred by what they had seen of the growth of the first modern Asian power. That powerful lady the Dowager Empress had died in 1909, leaving China open to civil uprising. As Jennie prayed in her room, she could hear gunfire beyond the city walls.

In the hospital not far away, Dr George Charter was also listening to the sound of fighting coming closer to the city. Reckless recruiting for the Republican army was turning it into little more than an armed mob, out for the blood of Manchus, and Dr Charter was aware that the north-eastern third of the city of Hsi-an-fu housed Manchu military families.

His little girl Dorothy was very ill; he and his wife had that day faced the fact that she was dying; but for a moment she was asleep and he left her side to walk through the hospital. In the decade following the founding of the MMA, hospitals had been set up in each of the three provinces where the BMS worked. They cared for a population frequently stricken by epidemics of smallpox, cholera and typhus, debilitated by drug abuse and prone to tuberculosis, afflicted by eye disease because of the dusty conditions of the dry months.

Here at Hsi-an-fu there were beds for thirty-two in-patients. There was an operating room where prayer was offered before each operation. There was an outpatients department, where the preacher for the day would talk to patients waiting to see the doctor.

Despite his sense of impending catastrophe, the mob outside, his little girl slipping away from him, George Charter smiled as he remembered the lively scenes often seen in the department. One day, as one of the mission staff had talked of a Saviour who had given sight to the blind and healing to those with leprosy, an objector had leapt up to challenge the speaker: 'But he doesn't do those things today.' From the back of the waiting room came another voice. 'Yes, he does,' it insisted. It was the voice of a man who had entered this 'Jesus hospital' blind and left, cataracts removed, with his sight restored. All the man knew was that once he was blind; now he could see. It had been a vindication of everything that the MMA stood for.

That night, 22nd October 1911, Charter was the only doctor in the hospital, with one nursing sister, Helen Watt. Dr Stanley Jenkins, after six years in charge of the hospital, was on furlough. Dr Andrew Young was on a medical tour of the hills in the north of the province. Dr Cecil Robertson had been visiting patients in the suburbs when the inner gates of the city had closed.

Those moments of reflection in the quiet hospital were the last that Charter was to have for many weeks. Suddenly the hospital was full of terrified and wounded people. The rebels had entered the city, seized an arms depôt in the southern suburb and distributed weapons to all who would use them against the Manchus. The Manchu area of the city was on fire; members of a Swedish mission had been killed.

As thousands of people, Manchu and Chinese, died in the city, hundreds more were dragged with bullet and stab wounds, burns and shattered limbs, into the hospital. Dr Cecil Robertson, desperately needed, had to be hauled on ropes over the closed city gates. Dr Andrew Young risked his life between the Imperial and Revolutionary armies to get back from the outer area of the province to the hospital.

In the wards and the operating theatre, 1,500 seriously wounded people were treated, while another 2,000 sought refuge within the hospital's walls, spilling out into courtyards and stables. Sir Alfred Pearce Gould, the distinguished English physician, was later to say that no London hospital could have coped with the demands made on that little hospital in northern China. There were demands on love and forgiveness as well as on stamina and skill. Amidst a group of terrified women who had sought refuge in the mission compound and in Jennie's school, Mrs Shorrock found the daughter of Yu Hsien, the governor who had ordered the massacre of mission staff in Shansi.

The struggle that was to result in the abdication of the Emperor in 1912 continued. A relief expedition led many missionaries to the relative safety of Peking. For Andrew Young and Cecil Robertson, however, there was no question of leaving Shensi. Cecil Robertson established field hospitals in the areas of the fiercest fighting. Desperately wounded men were carried on make-shift stretchers through the snow for what treatment he could give them with a few dressings, a handful of pain-killing drugs, and the help of an assistant provided by the Red Cross. Then they were sent on down to the packed hospital in the city.

Amidst the exhaustion of unremitting work and the sadness of watching those they could not save, there were still moments of encouragement for the Christian doctors.

'I am very glad we have remained up here', Cecil Robertson wrote to a friend. 'The soldiers seem very willing to listen to the Gospel just now. When I was going round late one night I found one man with three or four others round him. He was the only one who could read and he was reading the Gospel to the others.'

When Cecil Robertson established a hospital for permanently disabled soldiers, the Chinese called it 'The Pity the Wounded Hospital'. The service the missionaries had rendered to people on both sides of the conflict was to stand them in good stead in the chaotic period still to come.

*

In the years after the revolution and the formation of the Republic, China was almost torn apart in the struggle between warlords claiming power. Then came the 1914–18 war. China sent 100,000 men to France, often accompanied by missionaries who were able to act as a bridge between them and the strange western culture in which they found themselves.

Yet, through the upheaval, the Chinese Church was growing, both numerically and in self-determination. From 1919 to 1924, the membership of Protestant churches rose by between sixty and seventy per cent.

The spirit of reform sweeping the country was a spur to every area of mission, evangelistic, educational and medical. Literacy campaigns by the state offered opportunities in the production of Christian literature. A version of the Scriptures in 'popular' rather than 'scholarly' language had been produced in 1907 and the Baptist presses were busy with literature to accompany it.

Prison reform opened Chinese prisons to the Gospel. With the clamour for Western-style education, schools and colleges which had previously catered only for Christians and their children were suddenly in great demand by the general population. Such rapid changes were not without their heartaches, but who could doubt the evangelistic opportunities they offered?

Money from the Arthington Trust was used to start work amongst students, and was later handed over not only to the YMCA but also to the YWCA, for education was changing the life and expectations of Chinese women. The Shantung Christian University now incorporated ten missionary societies. It trained teachers for Christian schools, pastors and evangelists, arts and science graduates for government schools and colleges, doctors, nurses and pharmacists.

The Jenkins-Robertson Memorial Hospital opened in 1917 with 120 beds, four times the size of the original hospital where the two men had worked so devotedly. Both had succumbed to typhus within months of each other.

The Chinese Church itself was growing in confidence in

its own ability to be self-governing, self-financing and self-propagating. By 1922, at a meeting of the National Christian Conference in Shanghai, the majority of the 1,200 delegates, including the chairman, were Chinese.

So, for a heady and exciting period, the possibilities for growth seemed endless. By the end of the second decade of the century, Christianity looked set to play a major rôle in twentieth century China. Perhaps it was unrealistic to expect missionaries intent on seizing every opportunity that the Republic created, caught up in a fast-changing political and military situation, to read the signs of the times.

It is easier to read them with hindsight. A corpus of ideas at variance with Christianity – faith in reason and progress – was developing. The faith that motivated the missionaries was challenged by the growing numbers of radical intellectual students. Chen Duxiu, who was to spearhead the cultural revolution, pronounced that 'The value of a religion is in direct proportion to the extent of its benefit to society.' Ever since the days of Timothy Richard, Baptist missionaries, more perhaps than other Protestants, had stressed the necessity of a self-governing, financing and propagating church, a Chinese church. Nevertheless Western missionaries, for all their love and service to the people of China, still represented a culture that was not and never would be Chinese. Perhaps, with their educational methods, the missionaries had raised more questions than, with their theology and culture, they were able to answer. But which of us, in the early days of Republican China, would have been able to read the signs of the times? Which of us would have been able to assess the influence of the Russian Revolution, or to grasp the significance of the Society for the Study of Marxism, set up in 1918 in Peking?

6. Into the Shadows

Indian Subcontinent 1840 to 1930

There! Isabel Angus had written the word in her letter home and she would let it stand, even though that word, 'failure', glared accusingly up at her from the page and she knew that it would hurt and confuse those who read it.

It would have been easy to write a different, though less honest, kind of letter. She could have talked about the small successes, the new girls' school recently opened at Patna. She could have confined herself to describing the business of her own life, her oversight of women's work across a large area of North India. But those were not the thoughts that filled her mind tonight, and they were not the issues she had just been discussing with her colleagues.

It was 1922 and war had wrought many changes in the world. In China the changes were not yet so apparent as to dampen the hopes of the National Christian Conference there. But here in India everything was in turmoil. Gandhi's campaign of non-violent non-cooperation with the British formed the sole topic of conversation in army messes and at the dinner tables of civil servants. It occupied the conversations, too, of the missionaries.

'We were talking over present-day developments in India,' Isabel recounted in her letter, 'and we agreed about the failure which we as missionaries seem to have made, failure to inspire the Indian church to anything like the ideal we had hoped for, failure so to present the Gospel to the non-Christian world as to grip and touch it. At the close of my fourth decade here, this aspect of the situation comes vividly before me, but one asks *why* with honest intentions and desires for good – which I think we *can* claim – the lack of impress is so palpable?'

The questions were not in fact new to Isabel, though the careful expression of them was. 'Palpable lack of impress' – that, she knew as she read through her letter, had the ring of the experienced educated woman of sixty. But thirty years previously, in the small town of Bhiwani a hundred miles from Delhi, the young Isabel had felt 'failure' for the first time. Then her words had been wrung from her with passionate intensity.

'The whole fabric of the last seven years' work seems to crumble into dust as one touches any part of it. The School is at its last gasp; I have watched my best girls grow cold and callous in their homes, and we have not a single new enquirer among our pupils . . . I still believe that God has some purpose in it all and will still give a great blessing to Bhiwani . . . But the thing that half breaks my heart is – what no kind words from other people will do away with – the conviction that I go with all my dearest hopes unfilled and the very work which I so believed was going to be done unaccomplished.'

Unfilled hope. Unaccomplished work. What was it about North India that rewarded her missionaries with little more than that? In the South of India, Protestant missionaries had met with at least some response. But those working as the BMS did in the North had for over a century found little to rejoice in. They could hardly claim numerical success in a Baptist church membership that amounted to little more than a thousand, concentrated in three main areas – around Delhi in the North-West, around Calcutta and Orissa in the East and in Ceylon.

It had been the lot of the India missionaries to plough doggedly on in preaching and teaching with little human encouragement. They clung, as Isabel did in Bhiwani, to the belief that 'God has some purpose in it all', yet the purposes of God seemed strangely slow to manifest themselves. They felt that they needed far more resources of personnel and money for their task, yet were aware that the denominational spotlight had shifted from its first field. Sometimes, when they were tired and disheartened, it was almost hard not to resent the fact that the Jamaica mission had been crowned with popular success and that the excitement of the Congo mission had captured the imagination and fired the prayers of the churches at home.

So what was it about North India? India had two powerful religions. The BMS was one of the few missionary societies working amongst the Muslim population of India. The society's experience in that sphere was often sought by others, and the Welsh Baptist, Bevan Jones, had opened a school of Islamic Studies in Lahore. But in the main it was amongst Hindus that the BMS effort was concentrated, and it was the stranglehold of the caste system that had done so much to thwart their efforts and erode their hopes.

William Ward had referred to 'the chain of caste'. Although Hindus would listen politely to the preaching of the Gospel, that chain bound them so tightly as to make it almost impossible for them to respond to the good news.

A Hindu of caste who professed faith in Christ was immediately outcast from his community. He was at best disowned, at worst physically attacked by his family. He found himself with no home, no means of earning a living, and no emotional support other than that of the missionary himself and a handful of fellow converts who were like him always in danger of losing their tenuous grip on their new-found faith.

Despite efforts by the Home Committee to encourage India missionaries to move out of the market place and into the home, the thrust of their strategy had for decades remained where Carey had first placed it – on preaching in the bazaar. Such outdoor evangelism left few resources for the teaching and oversight of new Christians. Isabel Angus, working in Agra, had longed for more hours in each day for, she recognized, 'There is a need for as much work amongst the Christians as amongst the heathen.'

Such Hindu converts as there were were often of low or no caste. Hardly surprisingly, they leaned heavily on the missionary for physical, emotional and financial support. For the whole of the second half of the nineteenth century and well into the twentieth, that relationship of dependency had been a source of irritation to the Home Committee of the Society. The Committee, for reasons ranging from theological principle to financial constraint, wanted to see the independence of the Indian Baptist Churches. Yet all their attempts to encourage the infant Indian church to stand on its own unsteady feet had foundered on the rock of the protective stance of most missionaries and the dependent attitude of their converts. So, at sixty, Isabel Angus looked back over four decades and wondered if she and her colleagues had somehow got it all wrong. Yet somewhere inside the battle-weary woman was the girl of twenty who had with such high hopes and such sure faith given her life to Christ and to India. Not in fact to the BMS, which at that time did not accept women as missionaries in their own right, despite the work done by missionary wives from Hannah Marshman onwards, but to the Baptist Zenana Mission.

Isabel could not remember a time when she had not known and dreamed about the Zenana Mission, for her mother had been one of its founder members and then its Foreign Secretary. Somehow Mrs Angus, wife of Joseph Angus, BMS Secretary in the 1940s and then for nearly fifty years President of Regent's Park, a Baptist theological college, had found the time to teach her daughters the facts and the stories of the Zenana Mission. The fact that, if it was hard to reach the men of India with the Gospel, it was harder still to reach the women, shrouded in purdah or locked away in the zenanas, the female living quarters of wealthy Hindu homes.

For the little girl allowed to listen to visiting missionaries in the quiet rooms of the college or the sunlit garden of her home, and for the young woman encouraged to study languages at Bedford College and Greek with a Regent's Park tutor, it was hard to imagine the status of Hindu women, 'unwelcomed at birth, untaught in childhood, enslaved in marriage, degraded in widowhood, unmourned at death'.

Isabel had learnt, too, the stories that had tugged at her heart and provided a focus for her own Christian faith. How in the mid nineteenth century two India missionary wives, Elizabeth Sale and Marianne Lewis, had been irresistibly challenged to try to gain access to the zenanas of Jessore and Calcutta. How what they had found on their first tactful visits had provided them with a word-picture to put before the busy Baptist women of England, women for whom idleness was as great a horror as ignorance.

'The apartments of the zenana are usually dreary, ill-lighted, ill-ventilated and miserably furnished rooms, so constructed that their inmates may see as little as possible of the outside world . . . In some cases the number of women thus immured is very great . . . and having received no education, unable to read books, with no knowledge of any art or needlework, they are shut up in utter indolence. The survey of such jewels as they may possess, the care of their little ones and the discussion of any family gossip or of whatever items of news find their way to them from the outside world are their only amusements.'

Isabel was brought up on the story of how in May, 1867, twenty-five ladies had met together in the Mission House, for a while in John Street, London. Their meeting was presided over by a man, Dr Underhill, yet they had a sense of their own rôle because they knew that the women of India could be reached only by other women. There were other exciting stories, for the BZM had grown quickly, sending in its first fifteen years thirty-two Zenana missionaries to India to work alongside fifty Indian Bible women.

So the young woman who in 1880 had offered her service to the BZM had been the product of a loving family and of an unusually stimulating academic background leavened by missionary compulsion. Twenty-five years later Lilian Edwards, daughter of the Principal of the Cardiff Baptist College, was to tread the same path. Both these young women were schooled in the doctrines that kept at arm's length the new trend of theological liberalism. The application form of the BZM requested them to state those doctrines which they believed to be vital. Lilian had had no hesitation in responding with 'justification and sanctification'.

So a new generation of highly educated and deeply committed single Christian women had sailed as evangelists, teachers and doctors, first to India and then to China. In the work of the Zenana Mission, later incorporated into the BMS as the Women's Missionary Association, lay many of the roots of the twentieth century feminist movement. Meanwhile the Girls' Auxiliary, founded in 1903, began to prepare the next generation of girls for missionary service.

Yet what could fully prepare young English women for the culture of India, for the idols, the festivals, the cruelty, the famine and disease? isabel had begun her work in the relative security of Delhi. There zenana visiting was already well-established by the missionary wife, Harriet Smith, and three Zenana Missionaries. Yet, a hundred miles away, she knew, there was no education at all for girls in the town of Bhiwani. It was to her own mother as Foreign Secretary that

Isabel had to write for permission to go alone to Bhiwani to start work there. She would be the only European in the city.

So the young woman brought up in the theological college of Victorian London had rented rooms over a grain shop in one of the main bazaars of Bhiwani. From there, in the relative cool of each early morning, she had set off to explore its winding alleys, jostled by animals and by people whose rough dialect was far removed from the cultured Urdu she had learnt in Delhi. Full of the irrepressible hope that had not yet had to face failure, she had turned the stares of those who had never seen a European woman before to good account.

'I took advantage of the people's curiosity', she wrote home, 'to ask them where they lived and whether I might come and see them . . . Sometimes I go along a street and enter every open door I find, and ask the women whether I may sing tham a bhajan (chorus).'

Before long Isabel had set up a small school, convinced of the value of education in the process of evangelization. But, if she had come to India to teach, she soon found that there were other skills to be mastered. To Bhiwani came Dr Ellen Farrer, sent to India by the BZM before the Medical Missionary Auxiliary of the BMS had even been mooted. In the cramped dispensary that would one day be a hospital with a nurses' training school, Isabel had had to learn how to help Ellen with basic surgical procedures and the giving of medicines. Later when famine and plague struck and the chain of caste tied the hands of the Indians from helping one another, it was the hands of the woman missionary that had to comfort and heal.

If it was an indomitable woman who had cleaned up the wounds and confronted the plagues and taken her Bible into the zenanas, so it was a brave woman who dared to look back over her life's work and question whether she had got it right. But what Isabel knew that night was also how much courage had been required, not of the women who preached the message but of those who heard it. 'Oh, that I could be sure,' a Hindu woman had once cried to a missionary who had patiently visited her, 'whether what you say is true or not! Sometimes I think your words must be true; again I remember how ancient our religion is and how our forefathers have lived and died in it, and I say, it will surely do for me. And then, at other times, I feel so confused that I am tempted to give up all religion.' The path to Christian faith for an Indian woman was fraught with dilemmas and dangers. Yet, in the end, that Hindu woman had been courageous enough to acknowledge, as the Indian Bible-women who worked alongside the British missionaries had also acknowledged, 'You, sister, have grasped my hand and Christ has grasped yours.'

*

The *Students' Chronicle*, based first in 1902 in Dacca and later transferred to Serampore College, was aimed at the students of all five universities of India – Bombay, Madras, Punjab, Calcutta and Allahabad. That it was offered to them for a halfpenny a copy was thanks to a 'Helpers' Circle' of subscribers in English churches. Quotations in Arabic, Sanskrit and English on its cover indicated that it was intended for all, of whatever faith, who were 'sincere enquirers after the highest truth'. Yet its motto, emblazoned in Greek – 'To bring to a head all things in Christ' – left no doubt of the conviction of its editors as to where the search for the highest truth would lead.

Decades of BMS educational work by both men and women in India had been founded on the belief that enlightenment generally would surely point to Christian truth specifically. That it was only a matter of time and effort

– and 'honest intentions and desires for good' – before one issued in the other. The harsh lessons of the late nineteenth and early twentieth century was that that was not necessarily so.

In 1911, the India Field Secretary, Herbert Anderson, had recommended the closure of Baptist elementary schools in Ceylon. It had not been an easy decision and had felt like a betrayal of the work of Ebenezer Daniel who had revived the flagging schools set up by Chater and of the service of the missionary translator Charles Charter who had worked in the ancient capital of Kandy for three decades.

In the mid nineteenth century there had been a chain of about forty small schools, drawing children from the predominantly Buddhist Sinhalese population. The avowed aim of the schools had been not only to teach children to read but to introduce them to the Lord Jesus. Yet the village schools had foundered. They lacked money – and were reluctant to compromise their position by accepting government aid. They lacked trained Baptist teachers, for it was not until 1914 that there was a Baptist College in Colombo. Eventually, they lacked pupils. Though Buddhism was not as daunting to the missionary spirit as Hinduism was proving, Buddhist parents became alarmed when their children came home from school telling Bible stories and singing hymns.

To pull back from an area of work to which other people had given so much of their lives, to admit at last that word 'failure', was hard. Worse, it could be interpreted as lack of faith. Yet Herbert Anderson was aware that faith was also about stewardship, about putting limited resources where they were most effective. At the moment the need was for boarding schools for the children of those parents who had become Christians in the churches of Colombo and Kandy.

There had been other apparent failures. Certainly Serampore College, that flagship of Baptist education, had failed to find a rôle for itself in theological education. Cuttack Theological college, based at the heart of the Baptist community in Orissa, was training pastors for its churches. Serampore, on the other hand, had spent years in both academic and spiritual doldrums, while controversy over its rôle and future rocked the Society. If the college was failing to train the evangelists and pastors needed for the leadership of independent Indian churches, should it continue to be a drain on the resources of the BMS? On the other hand, was it possible, or too late, to re-establish its academic reputation as a Christian university born of the liberal vision of Carey, Marshman and Ward?

The view of some influential men in the Society, including Honorary Secretary Underhill and India Secretary Herbert Anderson, was taken up by George Howells, while he was on the staff of the theological college at Cuttack. The appointment of Howells as Principal of Serampore in 1904 heralded an era of academic influence and excellence for the college. But amidst the acclaim and success, questions remained. Serampore was undoubtedly now producing theological scholars; it was not providing the pastors and teachers needed to work with simple Indian Christians in small churches.

Meanwhile, influenced by the growing Student Christian Movement and YMCA, the BMS was exploring ways of working with Hindu and Muslim students in higher education. A rapid succession of very able men – Wright Hay, Sutton Page, William Carey (great grandson of the founder), Rawson and Bevan Jones went wholeheartedly out for the minds of the student population of Dacca. Alongside the *Students' Chronicle* and evangelistic campaigns headed by preachers from Oxford went more practical work. Hostels offering a decent, peaceful place to live and study became a haven for some students after the dirty overcrowded houses they had had to share in the brothel areas of the city.

Student work was not without its significance. Amongst those young men who were challenged by the Christian faith were some who went on to lead the Indian church. Wright Hay, the pioneer of student work in Dacca, was instrumental in the conversion of a young man called Bimal Ananda Nag, who was later to be one of the architects of the Bengal Baptist Union. Baptist missionary education and student evangelism did bring men and women from Hinduism and Islam to faith in Christ. But they came in their ones and twos. It was only in a couple of localized areas of North India and amongst tribal peoples that men and women were coming to Christ not in their ones and twos, but family by family, village by village.

*

They opened the first Baptist church in the Kond Hills at Mallikopari on the site of a former liquor store and within a stone's throw of the hill where less than a century before the tribal people of the Konds had offered human sacrifice.

Now the whole valley seemed alive. Monkeys and mynah birds chattered in the trees and below them the flowers-of-the-forest had spread a red velvet carpet on the ground. The new mud and thatch building had been garlanded with flowers, so that it was hard to recall how sinister a place this had once been. The Kond Hills, looming over the plains of Orissa, southwest of Cuttack, were at once beautiful and fearful. And it was fear – fear of the forces of nature that could deal drought and deluge, that could send tigers into the villages or strike whole communities with sudden disease – that had driven the people of the Panos and Kond tribes to offer their terrible sacrifices.

Today, 9th January 1923, the people were bringing offerings not of propitiation to some unknown evil spirit but of thanks to a trusted God. A little column of people filed up the valley with their gifts of rice, eggs, pineapple, as the children from the mission school, faces shining with excitement, sang their Kui hymns.

So many people had played a part in this day. The British army officers in the 1840s, who, when the barbaric practices of the tribes in the remote hills had become known, had snatched hundreds of children destined for sacrifice and brought them down to the Baptist orphanages at Cuttack, Berhampur and Pipli. The children themselves, grown up in the care of Christians and finding the love of God for themselves, who had had the courage to penetrate the jungle of the hills again as guides for John Orissa Goadby, first missionary to the Konds.

Later, others had played just as vital a part. In the 1890s Abiathar Wilkinson had recognized that the Kond people needed the Scriptures in their own language rather than in Oriya, for the hill people were not, and never would be, the same kind of people as those of the plains. His Kui version of Mark's Gospel had been a stepping stone to the later work of Oliver Millman in Kui books and schools.

So the joy and sunshine of that afternoon had been won by the patient work of a series of missionaries – not by any means an uninterrupted sequence – some of whom had laid down their lives and those of their children in the beautiful hills that were yet dangerous and disease-ridden places. In the end, the longed-for response had surpassed all expectations. Just nine years before, in 1914, Bisi, one-time witchdoctor, who for three years had suspended the practice of his dark magic because the Light of the World was slowly spreading into his life, had come for baptism. And he had not come alone that Easter Day, but bringing his wife, their son and his brother-in-law, a whole family of the resurrection. Then others had come, following the same pattern, family by family, until the bungalow of the evangelist Biswas could not contain them for worship and they had needed this first church building.

As the Christians, summoned both by drums and by a church bell given by an English congregation, assembled, there were others who watched from a distance, curious but unsure. It would be just four years before the village of Dombinaju gathered at the river for the baptism of forty-four of its people on Christmas Day and the taking of a new name, Kristian Kaju, for their village.

There were others who watched from amongst the trees, distanced by their own infirmity. There were those barely able to see because of cataracts; those dragging themselves along with infected wounds and sores; those weak from endless attacks of malaria or from tuberculosis. The mission staff from the station at Udayagiri, gathered at the infant church, glimpsed the movements in the shadows and knew that the joy of today could be even greater if only they could have the doctor they longed for. All around them the people of the Konds were turning away from the sacrifice and witchcraft to which they had looked for healing. Now they expected the missionaries to bring them healing instead. Every morning at Udayagiri came the call 'Ama! Aba! We have come for medicine!'

The Medical Missionary Auxiliary was now 'of age', and there was a women's hospital, admittedly in need of renovation after the years of war, down in the plain at Berhampur. Dr Fletcher Moorshead, Secretary of the MMA, had visited the Kond Hills himself and knew the desperate need for a hospital there. Yet still the need remained unmet. So much was happening here that was far removed from the world of Delhi, a thousand miles away. Light was coming to the people of the Kond Hills, the light of education and the light of Christian faith. Yet still an old man with cataracts could cry in vain: 'I am

getting into the shadows. Give me medicine that I may
see.'

★

If, in the 1920s, the tribal people of the Kond Hills were
turning to Christ in their dozens, up in the Lushai Hills, in
the far northeast of India on the border with Burma, the
tribal people there were finding faith in their thousands,
There, too, there was a great need for medical aid. But at
least, by the late 1920s, the people of the Lushai Hills,
otherwise known as Mizoram, received an annual visit from
the doctor from Chandraghona.

Dr Teichmann loved his visits to the Lushai Hills. They
offered him everything – the excitement of a journey that
made him feel young again; medical interest, for, though
the Lushai Hills were not that far from the Chittagong Hills,
there were fascinating variations in the medical conditions
of the people there; above all, the annual visits offered him
the spiritual encouragement of seeing that, amongst tribal
peoples at least, it was possible for the Gospel to be received
with enthusiasm in India.

He was able to start his journey to Mizoram on the
Karnaphuli river. The Karnaphuli, which had its sources in
the Lushai Hills, flowed past the hospital at Chandraghona
which had been built at the meeting place of the plains of
Bengal and the Chittagong Hills. But soon Teichmann's
launch had to be abandoned, for the forested mountains of
Mizoram were very high and the rivers cut by fierce rapids.
It was a journey of a week by canoe, horseback and on foot –
a journey that triggered many memories for the doctor.

His arrival at Chandraghona in 1911 to take over the
work of the new Arthington Hospital had been a shock.
There, in a place that was barely a village surrounded by
forest and swamp, had been the small new hospital building

with four wards for thirty-two patients. But the hospital
had been so designed that the only way of crossing from one
side to the other was through the operating theatre.

There was the now dilapidated dispensary, used for early
work by Dr Orissa Taylor, who had pioneered medical
work in the Chittagong Hills. But the bamboo walls were
being destroyed by white ants and a glance at the corrugated
iron roof had left Teichmann in no doubt that it would be
scorching in summer and deafening in the rains.

There was the missionary's bungalow, so shrouded in
mosquito netting that Teichmann promptly nicknamed it
'the meatsafe'. But it was perched high on a hill above the
rest of the hospital and Teichmann's heart sank at the
prospect of being called out in the night. What was more to
the point, however, was that the hospital was empty except
for a collection of 'Wants Boxes', parcels of bandages, soap,
pyjamas, sent from churches in England and dumped in the
operating theatre. There were to be no calls for there were
no patients. The Mogh people of the hills, for whom the
hospital had been planned, came to the weekly bazaar in
Chandraghona with their cotton, rice and bamboo, but they
kept a very wary distance from the hospital.

That was when Teichmann had taken to the dug-out
canoe, so that now the trip by canoe into the Lushai Hills
brought back those days as if they were yesterday. He had
taken with him on those first exploratory journeys an Indian
compounder, trained in basic medical care, who spoke
Moghi. Together they had toured the area, trying to gain
the confidence of the people and the smiles of the children
whose spleens were already distended by repeated attacks of
malaria.

Teichmann was frustrated by the process of learning
Moghi – his Bengali was of no help to him here – for he
needed the language quickly in order to dispel the fears of
the people. On more than one occasion he had persuaded a

would-be patient to come back to the hospital for treatment, only to see the man flee in terror at the sight of dressings being sterilized over charcoal fires and instruments over meths burners.

Yet gradually the people had begun to come so that until recently a trip like this into the Lushai Hills had been unthinkable. For seventeen years, until the arrival in 1928 of a second doctor, Jimmy Bottoms, and of the first European sister, Sister Timmins, Dr Teichmann had been unable to leave the work at Chandraghona. The hospital was often full to overflowing, not only with patients but with the families who came with them to prepare their food, for neither Hindu nor Muslim patients would eat food cooked by a Christian.

There were frequent epidemics of influenza, which could be deadly, and of cholera, needing intravenous saline injections. There was also the growing work amongst leprosy patients. When the first two leprosy sufferers had presented themselves at the hospital in 1913, Gottfried Teichmann had been at a loss. He himself was frankly afraid of leprosy, for like everyone else at that time he believed it to be highly contagious. Yet he knew that as a Christian he could not send the two men away. He housed them, and others who followed, on a hill apart from the rest of the hospital, and had fed and clothed them until they died.

Then, however, Teichmann had heard of the work of Dr Muir, a medical missionary in Kalna, who was convinced that leprosy was not an incurable disease. Teichmann had begun to see the possibility not just of offering leprosy sufferers Christian care but of treating them with hydnocarpus oil. The Mission to Lepers, as it was then called, had heard of his work and in 1926 had made a financial grant, so that now the leprosy work had a new site, a chapel and a small dispensary.

So the work at Chandraghona had for years taken all

Dr Teichmann's time and energy. Now, however, he had the help of Sister Timmins, who was training female nurses; with the breaking down of the purdah system, women patients were coming to the hospital for treatment. And now at last, there was the second doctor, leaving Teichmann free to make the trek to Lungleh in the Lushai Hills.

He was greeted by masses of people, eager for medical help. Some of them had conditions he did not often see in Chandraghona. Pulmonary tuberculosis was more common here in the larger and more settled villages of Mizoram than in his own area, and he saw patients with large goitres which he attributed to lack of iodine in the drinking water.

Exhausting as the journey to the Lushai Hills had been, demanding though it was to squeeze the work that could have kept a doctor busy for a year into one brief month, Gottfried Teichmann felt that he received from the Mizo people far more than he gave. At night he would listen to the singing of hymns coming from village after village perched on the top of the hills. The Mizos loved to sing. Once they had been warlike people, head-hunters, spirit-worshippers and then they had sung only when they were drunk.

Now, however, village after village in the Lushai Hills was becoming Christian. The work of the Welsh Presbyterian Missionary Society in the north of Mizoram and of the BMS, spearheaded by missionaries Lorrain and Savidge in the south, had triggered off a "people move-ment", in which thousands had come to faith in Christ. Since the beginning of the century, the two missionary societies had worked closely together. They produced a joint hymnbook for the Mizo people, soon outstripped by the people's passion for composing hymns. They complemented each other's work, with emphasis in the north on the training of pastors and evangelists and in the south on the translation of the New Testament. The early 1920s had seen the Lushai Hills alive with a spirit of joyful expectancy and response as not just the missionaries and evangelists but groups of new young Christians themselves went from village to village with the good news.

For the missionaries, it was hard to keep up with the pace of events, to baptize the newly converted, to teach the young Christians, to supervise a hundred small churches spread through the densely forested hills. These were the problems of success rather than of failure and Teichmann decided that they must be wonderful problems to have. His own work in Chandraghona had been challenging and often rewarding, in both medical and simply human terms. But there had been little spiritual encouragement, few converts to warm Teichmann's heart and reassure him that he was as much missionary as doctor. What he saw in the Lushai Hills seemed almost a different world from that of Chandraghona. It was a world in which a whole people, with its own culture, was turning to Christian faith.

On his last night in Mizoram, Teichmann was guest of honour at a farewell meeting. A blind man had composed a cantata on the first eleven verses of Paul's epistle to the Galatians. Next day, as Teichmann started the long trek home, it seemed as if he could still hear them singing.

*

The relationship between the two missionary societies working in the north and south of Mizoram was exceptional. Elsewhere the hundreds of Protestant missionary societies now working throughout the world regarded each other with attitudes ranging from the politely co-operative, through the warily tolerant to the frankly competitive. The growing need to plan together, to avoid treading on each other's toes, to agree aims and to share concerns and experiences was, however, drawing the societies together in organization and in conference. Two of the conferences in the early decades of the twentieth century related directly to issues of pressing concern to the BMS in India.

The World Missionary Conference of 1910 dealt with the thorny issue of the Christian approach to other religions. Experience in India had dispelled any idea that Christian mission there could consist simply of preaching to the heathen about sin and atonement and seeing him gladly accept the salvation of Jesus. Hinduism had proved both sophisticated and socially controlling. Baptist missionaries, while still believing that Christ was the way, the truth and the life and that no one came to the Father except through him, were forced to look again at the status they accorded to other world religions. Perhaps Timothy Richard had been ahead of his time in China thirty years previously, when he had appealed to the common ground of shared truth in his discussions with Muslims, Buddhists and the followers of Confucius. But now in India, Bevan Jones, the Baptist 'authority' on mission to Muslims, conceded that 'we shall rejoice in every evidence we can find of the presence of God's spirit in Islam.'

In 1928 the Jerusalem Conference of the International Missionary Council addressed itself to the question of the indigenous, autonomous church. That, too, had proved a protracted heartache for the BMS in India. The efforts of the Home Committee at the end of the previous century to encourage the infant Indian church to stand on its own feet had failed. Now other forces were at work.

The 1914–18 war had broadened the horizons of the Indian people. Nationalist protests against the Raj, sometimes bloodily quelled by the British, had refocused on the pacifist campaign of non-cooperation by Ghandi. From amongst the Indian church came voices like that of Bimal Ananda Nag, backed up by the influential William Carey of

Barisal, demanding that the Indian church be freed from the control of the missionary society and encouraged to find natural leadership from within itself.

Meanwhile with economic depression in England in the 1920s and 1930s, financial independence for the Indian church was increasingly desirable to the BMS. It was in this atmosphere of inevitable change that the Jerusalem Conference urged that national churches should be encouraged to choose their own identity and way of working.

John Reid, who had succeeded Herbert Anderson as India Field Secretary, came back from the Jerusalem Conference and looked at his field with fresh eyes. The Baptist churches of Ceylon, geographically separated and culturally different from the churches of North India, were, despite their small membership, already well on the way to independence. In 1895 they had set up a Baptist Union, a grouping of churches for mutual support. In 1935 the Ceylon Baptist Council would combine the Baptist Union, the missionaries and the Lanka Baptist Mission.

Thanks to the insistent pressurising of Nag and of Carey, there was also a Bengal Baptist Union that had been formed at Barisal in May 1922 but that had left the BMS missionaries still outside of church authority. 1935 would see church and mission fully integrated.

Orissa, benefitting from its clearly defined Baptist community, its theological college at Cuttack and the encouragement of events in the Kond Hills, was keen for independence. By 1933 it had its 'Sangha' working effectively. But the small scattered churches around Delhi and Agra were far less confident in their ability to make their own decisions and it was to be 1946 before the Baptist Union of North India was formed.

As the Indian church grew slowly and often painfully towards maturity, it was faced with opposition from ardent Hindus and the antagonism of nationalists who identified

Christianity with Western interference. Despite the dramatic response to the Gospel in localized tribal areas such as the Kond and Lushai Hills, Christians remained less than one per cent of the population of India.

Baptist churches had to come to terms not only with the 'palpable lack of impress' that had so disheartened Isabel Angus but with the positive hostility of religious and political forces. Meanwhile the international scene was changing yet again. The strength of the young Indian church was to be tested by another World War, which would issue in independence for India but at enormous cost. After the racial violence between Hindu and Muslim that culminated in partition, most of the Bengal Baptist churches were to find themselves not in India at all but in the newly created state of Pakistan.

7. Signs of the Times

China 1922 to 1952

The news from China in 1928 arrived in a grey London. For a wealthy handful of the young, life still had some tinselled sparkle. In the nightclubs of the West End, girls in cloche hats drank cocktails, smoked cigarettes in long holders and prepared for a riotous night with friends, rushing by cab from one jazz club to another until a giddy dawn.

But for the most of the population reality was very different. The rainbow bubble of euphoria and economic boom at the end of World War I had burst almost as soon as it had formed, leaving the aching realization of what had gone with the war. Gone was a generation, three quarters of a million sons, brothers, fiancés. Gone, too, were the markets for British shipbuilding, coal and textiles on which her pre-war prosperity and the livelihoods of whole communities depended.

As an alternating series of Labour and Conservative governments failed to find any way out of economic crisis, millions of people in work found their wages cut, while two million without work discovered the bleakness of life 'on the dole'.

The economic decline of much of the twenties that was to deepen into the Depression of the thirties cast its gloom over the desk of the Treasurer, John Broadley Wilson, in Furnival Street. The year 1925 had seen a deficit of £35,000 and overseas spending cut by £18,000. In 1926, the year of the General Strike, there had been a further deficit of £25,000. There were missionaries needing to be paid in

India, Congo and China. Yet many Christian churches in the north of England and in Wales were finding it difficult to respond to the needs of their own hungry communities. Although in the south-east, as Greater London sprawled ever outward, life was easier, church-going was in decline. For many families now 'religion' was found not in the pew but delivered by Canon 'Dick' Sheppard of St Martin in the Fields over the wireless set on the front room.

So it was in a grey Furnival Street that the China Sub-Committee received the latest grim news from Shantung, Shansi, and Shensi.

China had had her own legacy from the Great War – and it had taken the form of increased hatred of the Western powers. China had entered the war against Germany but at the Treaty of Versailles in 1919 had come out with nothing. The Allies kept their own pre-war concessions in China, their resented enclaves where foreigners, including some missionaries, lived in protected affluence unshared by millions of Chinese, and they allowed Japan also to keep her gains in China. Resentment against the foreigner and against the religious faith associated with him seethed. In May 1925 a demonstration by Chinese students, now a force to be reckoned with in Chinese society, ended in bloodshed and death, fired on by British and French military. Then the hatred spilled over with a fury that, within the next three years, would drive 5,000 of the 8,000 Protestant missionaries from their sphere of work.

'Christianity is the instrument of Western imperialism' was the slogan chanted at demonstrations and scrawled on walls. 'Missionaries are the running-dogs of Western capitalism.' They were slogans calculated to strike fear into the heart of the bravest and most experienced of missionaries. They were words that tore at the hearts, too, of thoughtful Chinese Christians. They clung to their faith; they loved their missionary friends and colleagues; yet they

could not fail to recognize that that faith and those friends
had for sixty years been buttressed in China by unequal
treaties and by force of arms.

The response of the BMS to events in 1925 had been,
along with other missionary societies, to issue a public
statement that they did not desire 'that the legal rights of
their missions and missionaries in China should in future
rest upon existing treaties between Great Britain and China,
and in particular upon the so-called toleration clauses in
those treaties dealing specifically with missionary work'.
Neither that resolution, nor the avowal by the missionaries
themselves that they had no political motive in coming to
China, did anything to reduce the anti-Christian activity,
which was especially ferocious in Shensi. What were the
missionaries to do?

There were compelling arguments in favour of their
withdrawal, not only for their own safety but for that
of their Chinese colleagues. They were not, after all,
indispensable, and Chinese leaders had been assuming
increasing responsibility in churches, colleges and hospitals.
On the other hand, who could doubt that as many skilled
medical hands as possible were needed in a country still rent
by rival military factions?

The Nationalist Party, the Kuomintang, led by Chiang
Kai-shek since the death of Sun Yat Sen, expelled the
Communist faction who wanted nothing less than the
complete transformation of society. Deprived of influence
in the cities, the Communists turned instead to the rural
areas where the old agrarian system was breaking down and
found the arms of the peasants open in welcome to them. It
was amongst the poor and the powerless in the villages that
the Chinese Communists established their first party cells
and waited for their moment to come.

During 1925—27, attacks on Christians forced the partial
evacuation of missionaries from all three provinces of BMS

work. There were, as before, those who refused to leave. Mrs Arthur Shorrock had with her husband found her life's work at Hsi-an-Fu. She had worked alongside the doctors in the operating room and overflowing corridors of the hospital in 1911. During the rapid growth of Christian education after the Revolution, she had been Principal of the girls' school in the city. From her, Chinese girls had gained a startling new insight into their own abilities as women and their own worth as children of God.

In 1926, the situation in Hsi-an-Fu looked so ominous that Dr Wheeler of the Shantung Medical School and Dr Harry Wyatt of Shansi evacuated the BMS women and children; all except Mrs Shorrock, who refused to leave, and died during the nine-month seige of the city to which she had given a courageous and faithful life.

Now in 1928, there were new dilemmas and difficult decisions before the China Committee in London. The mission education which had done so much to extend the horizons of hundreds of thousands of Chinese had itself become the focus of the anti-Christian movement. Even the Nationalist government had new requirements for schools and colleges. Some of them caused little heart-searching for the Committee: two thirds of governing bodies and all principals of schools and colleges were to be Chinese. But what about the requirements that all religious instruction be banned from primary schools and merely 'optional' in middle schools and colleges? Surely that struck right at the heart of mission education.

Perhaps it was time for the Home Committee to outline clearly the aims of education. They were, they concluded, 'to win the lives of the young for Jesus Christ; to give a Christian education, especially for the children of Christian parents; and to make some definitely Christian contribution to the educational system of the country'.

The educational system in China was clearly going to be

the subject of much prayer when the staff of Furnival Street gathered each day at noon. The most likely way ahead seemed to be to make the 'option' of religious education as attractive as possible to older students and to provide Christian teaching outside of school hours for the younger ones. In the meantime, there was clearly a need for a deputation from London to assess events in China for itself. So the Rev. Charles Wilson, who after a decade in Bengal had become Foreign Secretary of the Society, and William Parker-Grey left for a visit to China, from which they were to return 'saddened by the sight of empty residences, closed schools, and of other centres of work only occasionally used, due to the serious depletion of the staff'.

*

In July 1937 Japan launched an undeclared war on a China weakened by internal struggle and ill-equipped for war in the air. Peking was evacuated and the Chinese armies driven back to the Yellow River; by the end of the year, Japan had captured Shanghai and Nanking. While the League of Nations formally condemned Japan's actions, neither Britain, France nor the United States attempted to apply any sanctions. Neville Chamberlain resolutely refused to take any action that might embroil Britain.

As the Japanese advanced from the north and east, inflicting horrible suffering on people in rural areas, the Chinese population withdrew. Fifty million people trekked west, laying waste their own land in a 'scorched earth' policy. As in the migration to Shensi half a century earlier, families trundled their belongings, their children and their old people on wheelbarrows, but now they also packed the trains, clinging to doors and windows. Meanwhile the government began to move both industrial equipment needed for the conduct of the war and most educational establishments to the western provinces.

Among those on the move were many members of Christian churches and students at mission schools and colleges. In Shantung and Shansi, church leaders and missionaries were torn in different directions. Did they go to care for those who left or stay to support those who remained? Could flight be interpreted as cowardice? Or staying as collaboration? In the end, as five Christian Universities were amalgamated on the campus of the West China Christian University, most of the Chinese staff from Shantung Christian University moved there; the missionaries remained to care for those students who stayed in the province.

In the cities of Shantung, the missionaries came under aerial bombardment. Outside, in rural areas torn by Japanese soldiers and Chinese guerrillas wreaking vengeance on each other and on the terrified civilians, Chinese pastors struggled to care for village churches. Casualties from the countryside poured into the mission hospitals at Ch'ing-chou-fu, Chi-Nan-Fu and at Chou-ts'un, itself badly bombed.

In Shansi, BMS staff under air attack in Tai-Yuan-Fu were more concerned about the suffering of the Chinese in the north of the province. In an attempt to re-establish what had been the northern stations of the work, the Rev. and Mrs Ernest Madge made their way to Tai-Chou, and the Rev. and Mrs Victor Hayward to Hsin-Chou. It was a brave attempt, to be marked by tragedy. In May, 1938, Dr Harry Wyatt set out to take supplies to the Madges. He, his colleague Beulah Glasby and his Chinese chauffeur were shot dead by Chinese guerrillas who mistook them for Japanese.

In 1939, with China now divided into the 'occupied zones' in the northeast and south, and 'free China' in the north and west, BMS staff reluctantly left Shansi. They had become more of a liability than an asset to their Chinese Christian friends. The Japanese held them to be collaborators with Chinese guerrillas. Chinese Christians had been rounded up, tortured and interrogated.

As the missionaries left Shansi, they took their farewell of those whom they had first trained and then worked beside. Nurse Chang had been trained in the Women's Hospital but was now matron of the Tai-Yuan-Fu orphanage. Children were in her arms and tugging at her skirt as she promised the departing missionaries, 'As long as God gives me an orphan to care for, I will stand by.' As the years of war unfolded, she was not only to maintain the orphanage but turn it into the focal point of a growing Christian community, with seventy-two baptisms and a worshipping congregation of over two hundred.

There was plenty for the missionaries leaving Shansi to do, both in Shantung and in Shensi, overwhelmed with refugees since 1937. Before the Japanese invasion, Shensi province had been in the unenviable position of being divided between the Nationalists and the Communists, for whom it had been the end of the 'Long March'. In 1934, the Communists had been driven out of their base in Kiangsi province in the south. In an astonishing feat of physical endurance and propaganda, they had marched 6,000 miles on foot, fighting the forces of Chiang Kai-shek as they went and attracting to their cause intellectuals disaffected with the Kuomintang. They ended their march at Yen-an-Fu, the most northerly outpost of BMS work in Shensi.

The Japanese invasion had, however, brought together Nationalists and Communists in what was for the time being a united front. Shensi became packed with refugees from the north and east. Every mission compound and church became a centre for relief work, while medical work was transferred to the boys' school when the hospital was bombed. Children enrolled in mission schools. Nothing, it seemed, could keep the mission staff from responding to the ongoing need for evangelism, teaching and healing. Until, that is, Pearl Harbour was bombed, the British and Americans found themselves at war with Japan and the missionaries became 'enemy aliens'.

*

Now the year was 1942, one hundred and fifty years after William and Dorothy Carey and their babies had sailed with John Thomas for India, and life in Britain as well as in China had been turned upside down by war. In London, the nightclubs that had glittered for the few were shrouded by the blackout, and class divisions seemed of no consequence in a nation united by war. Fathers were in uniform, mothers with ration books queued for food, and bundles of confused children were evacuated from the capital.

The BMS headquarters in London had been bombed on the night of 9th September 1940. Attempts to establish temporary offices nearby were ended by another air-raid two weeks later. By the climax of the 150-year celebrations in October, only a skeleton staff remained in the damaged Furnival Street buildings, and much of the BMS administration was centred appropriately where the story had begun, in Kettering.

The loss of the Society's home added fresh urgency to the challenge that had been chosen to mark the anniversary – to raise an additional income of 150,000 guineas. The years of the Depression had left the BMS with a deficit to be erased. On a more positive note, it was intent on the development of a new sphere of work in each 'field', in improved training for missionaries and on much-needed pensions for retired staff and widows.

The 'big names' of the denomination marked the event in their own way. Paper rationing made publishing difficult, but Dr Townley Lord of Bloomsbury produced *Achieve-*

ment, a *Short History of the BMS*, and the editor of the
Missionary Herald, H. L. Hemmens, wrote a cantata, *The
Kingdom of Light and Love*. That cantata was performed at
the Northants Association Meetings in Kettering on the
Whit Weekend in May, a century and a half on from Carey's
'deathless sermon'. It was also performed by smaller but no
less enthusiastic church and Sunday School choirs up and
down the land. For the ordinary men and women of the
churches threw themselves into the celebrations with a
determination more poignant perhaps than that which had
marked the centenary in 1892 when anything had seemed
possible: when the *Peace* had her base at Bolobo to open up
the Congo and the China missionaries were just moving
into their third province of work.

Soap rations were swapped for margarine ones as Baptist
women took up the idea of 'Widow Wallis tea parties'.
Fourteen friends would gather together to recall the
beginnings of the society, the more dramatically-inclined
taking the parts of Sutcliffe, Ryland, Fuller, and raising for
the BMS that sum of £13.2.6 that had been placed as a
pledge in a Kettering snuff box.

The 'Missionary Wants Box' was, and for three decades
would remain, a focus for the work of Baptist women.
They knitted, sewed, and found it in their hearts to be
generous in spite of the shortages at home. They were
rewarded with letters addressed to them personally or, like
this one, sent to the *Missionary Herald*.

'Always welcome, three boxes which arrived recently
were doubly so because we have had none for so long.
These had in fact been two years on the road held up by war.
What excitement unpacking and wondering all the time
what lay next and what under that. There were baby clothes
and toys, which bring delight to the Women's Hospital.
There were innumerable pyjamas which comfort the men.
Towels of all sorts, always useful, as are also pillow cases

and bandages. Some of the bandages were made of cloth that was a little too stiff . . . There were picture cards of Bible scenes that the evangelist finds a wonderful introduction to illiterate and young patients . . . What a difference between cold charity and warm Christian love, what a difference between the Mission hospital where economy always reigns supreme and the one where the little amenities of life create a generous and homely spirit. When you are buying little extras to make things look nice, don't forget our whitewashed walls.'

So the 150-year celebrations passed off in a plethora of Carey films, stamp albums, tea parties, Sunday School choirs – and some very real and sacrificial giving. They were barely over when news arrived from China. In common with other British and American nationals, the BMS staff of thirty-four missionaries with eighteen children in the Japanese-controlled area had been interned in March 1943 in camps mainly around Shanghai.

The missionaries were classed as 'civil internees', rather than as prisoners of war. But ahead of them lay two and a half long years of camp life, in overcrowded dormitories with restless children, with poor food and hygiene, and with endless physical duties to perform each day. There had been little mutual liking or respect between the business community and the missionaries; now the two groups were thrown into intimate and often tense proximity. But there was much call on the medical and other skills of the missionaries in the camps. They cared for the sick; they encouraged the anxious; they organized activities for frustrated children and teenagers; they conducted worship and Bible study. They were sustained all the time by the prayers of those thousands of miles away who, despite their own sorrows and privations, could not let go of the ropes.

In a Northampton church, three decades later, Miss Emily Pentelow, who had been on the staff at Tai-Yuan-Fu before being interned by the Japanese, sang every hymn with her hymnbook unneeded in the pew. In the prison camp, she had learned by heart the words of every hymn in the Baptist Church Hymnal. That eloquent testimony to her captivity was the only one that she would ever give; of those two and a half harsh years of her life she would otherwise say nothing.

At the end of the war the BMS resumed work in China with high hopes. The missonaries, who had been released from internment in September 1945 had had time to recuperate and also to think and study in England. They went back to China with an updated concept of mission. Events had forced them to redefine the role of the missionary and his relationship with the host country. They recognized as never before the need for the church in each culture to find its own distinctive expression of the Gospel. Ahead of them they saw not a resumption of the old ways but a fresh challenge.

And they were heartened and humbled by reports of the courage and faithfulness of the Chinese Church in their absence. Although most of the BMS staff, released from the camps, had gone to convalesce in England, others had been anxious to return at once to former areas of work and to re-establish contact with their Chinese colleagues. The Rev. Fred Drake and Mr Ernest Phillips in Shantung and the Rev. Eric Sutton-Smith and Mr Ralph Dart in Shansi found Chinese Christian pastors, teachers and dcotors who had shown amazing tenacity and compassion through years of national chaos and personal deprivation. With such leaders for the church, there seemed so much to hope for.

And so much to do. In Shensi Dr and Mrs Stephen Henderson-Smith and Sister Grace Stageman found the Hsi-an-Fu hospital in ruins. Churches in a bruised and battered Britain dug into their pockets to raise money for a hospital they would never see, and by 1948 there were 900 outpatients a day in the rebuilt hospital and sixty nurses, under a Chinese Principal, in the Training School. Meanwhile at San-Yuan, the Rev. and Mrs Mudd were helping to train pastors at the Bible Training School. As events were to turn out, those pastors within three or four years would be faced with full responsibility for the Chinese church.

In Shansi, Nurse Chang had kept every word of her promise. The children in the Tai-Yuan-Fu orphanage had known fear and they had known hunger but through it all they had known love. The church was not only alive but well, and rejoiced in 1947 in forty-four baptisms. The British Red Cross helped Dr and Mrs Handley Stockley and Mrs Madge to restart medical work in a hospital left in disarray by the Japanese invaders.

Shantung, with its larger and more well-established churches and educational institutes, had had more to lose than the other provinces. And it was in Shantung that it first became apparent that the hopes with which the missionaries had returned to China were to be short-lived. With the surrender of Japan, the 'united front' of Kuomintang and Communists had broken down. Attempts in 1947 and 1948 to restart Baptist work in Shantung province were thwarted by the fact that the area was a battleground between the Nationalists, who disappointed Christian leaders by becoming increasingly totalitarian, and the Communists.

In Spring 1949 the Communists, now led by Mao Tse-tung, routed their opponents, a remnant of whom retreated to Formosa. October 1949 saw the establishment of the People's Republic of China. Now Marxist hostility to religion reinforced the suspicion towards Christians and missionaries who had tended to show support for the Nationalist cause. Although it was not immediately apparent, it was the beginning of the end of religious freedom and mission in China, though miraculously not, as we now know, the end of the Chinese Church.

The Chinese Church was not initially afraid of Communism. Instead it began to ease itself free of its missionary connections. In 1949 a letter from Chinese Christians arrived on a the desk of the BMS Secretary in the new headquarters in Gloucester Place. It had been sent to the Boards of all the Missionary Societies working in China.

'The new era is the culmination of a century's struggle against external exploitation and centuries of internal feudalistic oppression . . . From now on a new political concept, a new philosophy, a new creed and a new mode of living will be instilled into the mass of the people. Much of China's traditional heritage will be scrutinized and, if need be, discarded . . . Likewise much of Western culture that has been introduced in recent years will be re-examined and shorn of its undesirable elements.

'We Christians in China feel the urgent necessity of re-examining our work and our relationship with the older churches abroad in the light of this historic change in China. We need not re-examine our faith for our fundamental faith in Christ is not to be shaken, and under the New Democracy, freedom of faith is definitely stipulated . . . It is also needless for us to relate here what the Christian movement in China has accomplished nor what share our Christian friends have contributed to that achievement . . .

'The future contribution of the missionary will lie along lines of special service projects and not along administrative lines. TO BE, TO SHARE and TO LIVE will be a significant contribution in itself.'

Just one year later, the mood changed. The Korean War was seen as an American threat to China. The attitude of the Communist Party towards the Church swung from consultation and toleration to suppression. The National Christian Council of China, the YMCA, the Christian Literature Society and individual denominations became the subject of condemnation. In a terrifying 'denunciation campaign', individual Christians were hauled before 'People's Councils' for trial and punishment. Panic-stricken Christians denounced each other for 'imperialist' or 'reactionary' attitudes.

The days of deputation to China were over. The China Sub-Committee was dependent for information on such letters as could be got out of China. In May 1951 Ernest Madge tried to convey the atmosphere of terror:

'How exactly does Communism transform the life of a community in the way it has done? Many familiar with Chinese patterns of living and political history must be at a loss to understand how Communism has obtained a stranglehold on all Chinese life and unified the country in a way that no other government has ever succeeded in doing . . . The answer is in the use of the psychology of fear . . .

'Even the accusation meetings have a technique of their own, designed to increase the fear in men's hearts and divide and redivide the population until every man stands alone, afraid to trust anyone, even those of his own family . . .'

Yet the missionaries were honest and objective enough to recognize the positive achievements of the new regime. 'After all this,' Ernest went on, 'is there any good to be said of the People's Government? Yes, there is, and very important things too . . . The law is now respected which it never was before . . . Finances are stable in China now . . . Prices have dropped dramatically and real wages, especially for the poor, have increased.'

The writing was on the wall. 'I am personally convinced', the Rev. Victor Hayward wrote in May 1951, 'that as far as internal conditions are concerned, the new regime has definitely come to stay for the foreseeable future. Historically speaking, I am sure that there has been no alternative. The new government is making ever greater achievements, at increasing spiritual cost.' Within months, Victor Hayward was to find himself not in China but in the corridors of Mission House.

For, during 1950 and 1951, it became clear to the BMS staff that it was in the interests of the Chinese Church that they leave. The very last to leave, in September 1952, was the China Secretary, the Rev. H. W. Spillett. For three years he had stayed in Shanghai to supervise the safe withdrawal of mission staff and the handing over of mission property to the Chinese Church. The only British missionary left in Shanghai, he had acted as minister to Holy Trinity Cathedral there.

In October, Mr Spillett stood before the China Committee in London. His heart ached for China, as the hearts of every missionary had ached as they left. But 'I have', he told his hearers, 'sound reason for believing that, despite years under Communism, the Christian Church will survive and emerge purer and stronger.' They were prophetic words.

But where now for the missionaries? Twenty-nine were ready for retirement or work at home. In 1952 fifteen former members of the China staff were transferred to India and Pakistan, and three to Ceylon; three went to Congo and two to Trinidad. Nine took a furlough while they prayerfully considered their future. Amongst these were the Rev. Arthur and Mrs Kathleen Elder. Where, they needed to know, did the Lord want them now? They were to be given their answer not when they were on their knees, but when they were standing in a queue for lunch at a Congress of the Baptist World Alliance.

8. Fruit that Endures

Congo and Angola 1914 to 1961

It is perhaps significant that the most settled period of missionary work in Congo – the period between the two World Wars – coincided with a time of rapid change in the country. All of us love to feel needed – and there was no doubt that the educational and medical skills of the missionaries were in great demand. While Portuguese Congo, now Angola, retained its predominantly rural character, the 1920s and 30s saw the growth of towns in the Lower River area of Belgian Congo. Further upriver, large companies were establishing plantations producing coffee, cocoa, palm oil, rubber or cotton, precipitating rapid social change.

Other factors beside the heart-warming assurance of being 'needed' made it possible for missionaries to spend years, sometimes decades, on one station. The years of terrible loss of life in Congo were over. Much had been learned about how to dress, house oneself, travel, survive in Equatorial regions. The BMS hospitals at San Salvador, Bolobo, Yakusu and later in 1936 at Pimu and in 1938 at Ntondo provided health care for Europeans and Africans alike.

Despite the need for teachers, doctors, nurses – and in the 1920s nearly a quarter of the doctors working in Congo were Protestant missionaries – the Roman Catholic administrations of both Belgian and Portuguese Congo had mixed feelings about Protestant missions. In the 1920s they gave huge subsidies to Roman Catholic schools and hospitals while offering little to help the work done by Protestants – this at a time when recession was tightening the belt of the BMS.

In Angola relationships between mission and state were particularly strained. The *Decree* 77 published in 1921 stipulated that schools were to be headed by Portuguese nationals and that the native African languages were not to be used except in public worship. After lying in abeyance for some time, this decree was to cause turmoil in the Angolan mission schools in the 1930s. At the same time, the Portuguese authorities moved to prevent would-be pastors and teachers from Angola crossing the border into Belgian Congo to train at Kimpese. Perhaps, however, 'competition' with the Roman Catholics kept the Protestants on their toes. Certainly it caused a rethink of educational priorities in the 1930s under which the institution at Kimpese was renamed 'L'Ecole de Pasteurs et D'Instituteurs' and offered two separate courses in teacher training and in theological and pastoral studies.

Despite the uneasy relations with the state, a network of station, village and regional mission schools spread throughout Congo. Village after village had its little school, a grass roof supported by poles or mud walls, presided over by a young teacher-evangelist who also led worship on Sundays. For two hours a day, five days a week, the sound of singing rose from the schools as thousands of children learned to read, write, add up and retell the stories of the Bible.

For the young village evangelist himself, the highlight of the year was to be collected by steamer for a refresher course at the nearest mission station. Otherwise these young men were on their own. Their horizons had been tantalizingly opened by basic education. They had glimpsed the clean, ordered and Godly life of the mission station. Now they had to struggle to practise what they had learnt in remote, filthy villages, still under the sway of the witchdoctor and of the superstitious old women of the community.

If he was fortunate, the teacher-evangelist had the companionship of a young Christian wife, trained in basic midwifery. That some of these young men gave up the struggle or lost their Christian faith or at least took their lucrative skills elsewhere, is not surprising. That many of them did not do so but formed the backbone of the mission's work in both education and evangelism was proof of their faith and integrity.

*

Without doubt, the educational 'showpiece' was Yakusu. But then, Yakusu had William Millman, whose brother Oliver was busy establishing education in the Kond Hills of India. Yakusu in William, also had a brilliant educationalist – and it had him for forty years, from the beginning of the century through to 1937. Forty years in which the Yakusu church grew from nothing to 5,000 members. Forty years in which Millman established schools, first for boys and girls, then for station workers, then for teacher-evangelists who needed to learn French, hygiene, agriculture, Scripture and how to preach. It was an education system that touched and changed the lives of 25,000 people.

Yakusu also had Edith Millman, a redoubtable lady. Married first to a pioneer missionary William Stapleton, Edith had had no choice but to return to England when he died, for missionaries' wives were not missionaries in their own right. Her second marriage, to Millman, however, opened the doors for her to return to Yakusu.

When Edith set up an afternoon school for the wives of station workers, it proved a noisy affair. The babies perched on the young women's laps grabbed at the writing implements they were trying to hold as they struggled to

form their first letters. Edith had an answer for that. Before
long there was a kindergarten, a 'babies' house' in the shade
of a large tree, with dolls and picture books, and outside it a
small garden with tiny spades. The flowers grown there
were taken to the sick people in the hospital. The sand-tray
used for play from Monday to Friday (except when it rained
hard, in which case it became a lake for toy boats) was used
on Sunday to illustrate the Bible story.

Surprisingly – or perhaps not – this formidable lady
herself resisted the coming of the single woman missionary.
Though single women were appointed to Congo, they
received less ready acceptance there than in India, so that
there were always more boys than girls in the schools and
more men than women in the churches. Yet perhaps even in
the 1930s women did have to have a touch of the
'formidable' about them to survive in Congo. There were
few words more sweetly damning of another woman than
that little phrase slipped into a letter or whispered from one
missionary wife to another at a conference – 'But she's not
very *strong*, is she?'

Still, Yakusu was particularly blessed. In the 1920s and
30s it did not only have William Millman. It also had
Clement Chesterman.

*

The steamer in the middle of the river gave four short blasts,
bringing the people running to the bank with their palm
branches and flags. He had come. They had prayed for a
doctor for Yakusu and he had come. They watched as the
station whaleboat was launched to take the Rev. C. Pugh,
the senior missionary, out to the steamer to take off his new
colleague. It was swiftly followed by an enormous canoe,
the grinning paddlers singing an enthusiastic boat song. But
when the doctor and his wife, after three weeks coming up

river on the steamer, stepped gratefully ashore, the cries of welcome held a note of amused amazement. At six feet four inches, Clement Chesterman was the tallest man the Africans had ever seen. He was to be Bondombe – 'the biggest man'.

As the huge man strode through the wards of the hospital and tried out his tentative Lokele in the teeming bustle of outpatients, trying to orientate himself to this country and this people after his Middle Eastern service as an army doctor in the 1914–18 war, never far away was a diminutive boy, Sunday. He was ten years old, and the tattoo down his nose showed that he came from Lokele fisher folk. In fact, such was the pace of change in Congo, Sunday's grandparents had been cannibals but now ate fish and bananas instead. Sunday was Chesterman's 'personal boy'.

So when the doctor decided that it was time to take his medical skills beyond the river bank and into the forest, Sunday was bound to go too. From the cases that came to him in the hospital, Chesterman was in no doubt that not only hideous accidents but preventable diseases ravaged the lives of the people who hunted food or scratched at the ground to grow plantain or cassava in isolated villages. He had seen malaria in the Middle East. But if, as he suspected, he had a fight on his hands to bring health to this area of upper Congo, he had to find out precisely what he was up against.

For two to six weeks at a time, Chesterman left the mission station for a 'medical itineration' that was in fact a trek, by dug-out canoe, by bicycle, on foot across streams and swamps and along narrow trails in the green twilight and soaking heat of the forest. Sunday was always glad when they reached a village and the doctor persuaded the chief to line up the people, while Sunday helped set up the folding table, the boxes of drugs, the microscope.

Chesterman started his sessions, which were times of
discovery as much as treatment, with prayer, but he swiftly
learnt that the people would not close their eyes for fear of
something happening to them while they were not looking.
It was hardly surprising if they believed the world to be full
of malevolence. They brought to the doctor babies who had
fallen into the fire, old women with huge ulcers. There were
endless cases of malaria, impetigo, intestinal parasites and
there were dozens of children in whom the hookworm
larvae had penetrated the soft skin between their toes as they
washed and fished in the river.

None of that surprised the doctor. But what he had not
expected, in his wildest estimates, was the terrifying extent
of sleeping sickness. As much as a third of the population of
the area showed signs of the deadly disease spread by the
tsetse fly, affecting the brain and spinal cord. As he saw the
early signs of infection, Chesterman knew that untreated,
the patients would degenerate through fever, mania,
lethargy and emaciation to death.

It took Clement Chesterman four years of medical census
between 1920 and 1924 to establish the horrifying prevalence
of sleeping sickness in the area. When he communicated his
findings to the Belgian authorities, their attitude to financial
help for BMS work changed as they ranged themselves
alongside him in the determination to conquer the disease. It
then took just three years' use of the drug tryparsamide to
reduce the level of infection to one per cent of the
population. The success was astounding. International
attention was drawn to the mission station in the heart
of Africa. The Rockefeller Institution offered financial
support. The Belgian authorities urged Chesterman to turn
his attention next to the oozing, raspberry-like lumps that
were the evidence of yaws.

But, if Clement Chesterman was winning his fight, he
was not doing so single-handed. Of far more significance to

him than the help of the Rockefeller Institute was the little army of young Africans in khaki shorts and white shirts who fought with him. Sunday was one of the first of the 'infirmiers', trained at Yakusu to combine the functions of first-aider, nurse, pharmacist and public health officer.

Unlike many BMS hospitals, where the work was restricted every time the doctor in charge went on furlough, Yakusu was fortunate in having, from the mid 1920s onward, two doctors. Fees from the treatment of European patients helped to fund the public health programme and the training of the infirmiers in anatomy (they had a coloured wall chart but how they needed a skeleton!) physiology, pharmacology, laboratory work, surgery and nursing. Alongside the lectures and practical experience in the hospital, the infirmiers also learnt how to teach the good news of Jesus who willed for men and women not only physical healing but the wholeness of salvation. Every young man accepted for training had to be either a church member or a definite 'enquirer', who had decided to be a Christian and was awaiting baptism.

As Chesterman had finished work on the wards one morning, Sunday had sought him out in a state of greater agitation than the doctor had ever seen in him.

'The drums, they are calling me,' he explained desperately, 'and I don't want to go.'

The drums were those preceding the initiation rites in the forest that marked the transition from adolescence to manhood. It was a time of decision for Sunday. This way? Or that – into the fullness of life of the Christian?

On the day Sunday was baptized, he took a new name, Victor. In fact he still had much to overcome. On the completion of his training in the infirmiers' school, he had to leave the security of the mission station to run a village dispensary sixty miles away. Equipped with his microscope, basic drugs and a handbook of tropical medicine, he was to be the sole exponent of modern medicine within a radius of fifty miles. In the halting French he had also had to learn, he would have to deal with plantation owners, state officials and soldiers. For him, as for dozens of other young men at health posts and dispensaries in the forest, on the river bank and on plantations, the task took every ounce of his Christian faith as well as every medical skill he had learnt from Chesterman.

But they did overcome. In the mid 1940s, Clement Chesterman who had returned to England in 1936 to replace Dr Fletcher Moorshead as Medical Secretary of the BMS, went back to Yakusu. He found seventy student infirmiers, as well as female nurses, in training. He found Sunday, the lad from the fisher folk, in charge of a health centre on a large plantation. He found that sleeping sickness was almost unheard of, that 50,000 cases of yaws had been treated in the twenty-five years since his steamer had first brought Yakusu in sight, and that epidemics of smallpox were a nightmare of the past.

*

A researcher looking at the pattern of church growth in Congo between the wars would quickly see that a period of adjustment after the 1914–18 war was followed by a lull caused by the economic constraints of the mid 1920s and then by sustained growth in the 1930s. Within this overall pattern, however, the life of the churches was often akin to the process of an incoming tide; a noisy rush up the beach, followed by a quiet slipping back before the next forward surge. For every group of keen new Christians, their time in the enquirers' class behind them, who made their joyful way to the river for baptism, there would be a smaller group 'disciplined' by their fellow church members and removed from the church rôle until their lifestyle came nearer to their profession.

The missionaries looked for evidence that their converts were 'new creations in Christ'. For western missionaries in the 1930s that meant fidelity within marriage, sexual restraint outside of it and no alcohol. But there were complex personal and ethical problems relating to the bigamy traditionally practised in Congo. If a man with more than one wife became a Christian, what was he to do? Put aside his 'surplus' wives so that he could become a member of the church, knowing, as the missionaries also knew, that ahead of them would lie destitution or prostitution?

Life in Congo was lived in the open. No African church member could keep details of his personal life secret in the way that, during the Victorian era and even beyond, some English church-goers had become so adept at guarding theirs. So before the church members' meetings in Congo were brought members who had committed adultery, beaten their wives or when drunk had become embroiled in fighting.

On the other hand, there were Congolese Christians who really were 'new creations' and had faithfully remained so for many years. Many of the 'boys' of the pioneer missionaries were now loved and respected elder statesmen of the churches. It was a great source of joy to Nlemvo, Bentley's first convert, when a new mission station south of the rail centre of Thysville in Lower Congo was named Kibentele after his beloved Holman Bentley.

The growth of the church at Kibentele was tremendous, from 500 members in 1920 to over 1,500 four years later. Then came the slipping back of the waves on the beach, a period of decline, to be followed by further growth. Rapid numerical growth itself brought problems, for it was impossible for mission staff to teach and care adequately for

new Christians. But for many young Christians Nlemvo
proved a 'father in God'. He was the first Congolese national to receive a Gold Medal from the Belgian
King for 'a life of modest labour, of fidelity and of
devotion'.

At Mabaya in Angola there was heart-warming evidence
of faithfulness of a different kind. This remote area of
Angola had been chosen for a new station to commemorate
the Silver Jubilee of the mission in 1903. It had, however,
proved a disease-ridden, hostile and finally impossible place
to work. Would be 'enquirers' faced torture and death. Just
two women had been brave enough to be baptized. When
the station was abandoned in 1915, its keys were handed to a
sympathetic caretaker. That elderly man and the one
Christian in the area had guarded not only the property but
the little glimmer of Christian insight they had been given.
They guarded it until they themselves believed that the
people of the area, now with a coffee plantation, were ready
to hear the Gospel again. Then they asked the mission to
return. The old site proved unsuitable for use but Arthur
Lambourne and his sister, Jessie, came in 1932 to nearby
Bembe. In four years they found themselves with a church
of over 500 members, with 2,000 enquirers and a school of
200 children.

Nlemvo and his contemporaries had been trained in
Christian ways, albeit European Christian ways, by living
closely with the early missionaries and travelling with them
to England on furlough. Now, as the paternalistic attitudes
of the early years began to modify towards what would one
day be a recognition of partnership, a new generation of
church leaders was receiving a different kind of training at
EPI, Kimpese.

While many of the more gifted young men chose to take
the teachers' rather than the pastors' course, Kimpese
helped to produce church leaders of the stature of Jacques

Nzakimwena. Leaving Kimpese in 1936 for two years experience in the oversight of sixty villages in the Ngombe district, Jacques returned for further training at Kimpese and ordination. He then had twelve years' ministry in the Lower Congo, and was instrumental in bringing many people to Christ. A year before his death from cancer in 1956, he represented Congolese Baptists at a Baptist World Alliance Congress in London.

But while Jacques trained at EPI in the mid-1930s, the person everyone was talking about and writing about in the pages of the *Missionary Herald* was Botendi, the lad who sparked off the revival at Bolobo. As roads began to be opened up in other areas of Congo, and as medical itineration from Yakusu by dug-out and foot was replaced by motor launch and motorbike, Bolobo remained cut off except by river. But Bolobo was prosperous. The engineering works started in the days of the *Peace* and, later, carpentry and cane work and trade in ivory with the river steamers had made for a wealthy community. They had also produced a materialistic and spiritually apathetic attitude in the Bolobo church. The 1929 station report recorded 139 baptisms, but 149 suspensions. In 1930 the Rev. Andrew McBeath started a Bible school for boys. His letters to England urged prayer for spiritual revival at Bolobo. In 1934 it came.

One night Botendi put down his book, *Sammy Morris, the Kru boy who sought the fullness of the Holy Spirit*, and had a dream of lost sheep. The effect was so overwhelming that he not only recommitted his own life to his Lord but challenged his young friends in the carpentry shop to confess how careless they too had become to their Christian life.

The following Sunday thirty-six young men went forward during the Sunday worship as a sign that they wanted to recommit their lives. The usually dull Monday evening meeting came alive with testimony to the power of the Holy Spirit. Groups of revitalized young men set off to preach in the villages along the river. Before long the church building at Bolobo was full to overflowing on Communion Sundays, when people came from surrounding churches, and separate services were held for children and for the hospital patients.

The revival spread even to the old women, most steeped in superstition, and the fetishes that had showed that they wanted it both ways were finally flung into the river. The evidence of the Bolobo revival was seen not only in 700 baptisms in 1936 and in a doubling of the church membership from 2,000 to 4,000 between 1934 and 1938 but in a changed spirit in the whole community. Young men who had been stealing from the workshops made redress. Feuds were made up. Young teachers who had had an exalted opinion of themselves lost their conceit and the services that started each day's work in the hospital, enjoying a settled period under Dr Ian Acres, held a new note of praise.

*

Yakusu snapshot 1937. They are dedicating the new church building today, thirty-five years to the day since the baptism of the first convert at Yakusu. The Communion Table has been given by a church in a place called Worthing. Curious African faces – not part of the Yakusu congregation, just curious – peer through the Gothic windows. Inside small children present (Millman's words) 'a little tableau. Standing in lines to represent the cruciform plan of the church, and joining hands together to show the roof, while four of the bigger children hold a pole to represent a spire, they sing their special hymn – 'building the house of the soul under the direction of Jesus'.

Somewhere a few thousand miles away, leading lights of the missionary societies are provisionally talking over the agenda for the International Missionary Conference (IMC) to be held at Madras in 1938. Top of the agenda: styles of worship for an indigenous church.

*

The 1939 war began in an arena so far removed from the world of the carpenters' workshop on the banks of the great Congo river that it was hard to imagine how one could possibly affect the other. But in 1940 Hitler invaded Belgium. There was a clamour for the raw materials in which the Belgian Congo was rich, pushing the process of industrialization which had begun in the 30s into top gear.

Young Congolese men – perhaps Botendi, or were his joiner's skills needed for the war effort? – found themselves in uniform bound for East or West Africa, the Middle East or Burma. They came back with new ideas from abroad and a desire for change at home. Meanwhile, Belgian nationals had come to work in Congo and in 1942 won the right to form Trades Unions, a right extended at the end of the war to Africans.

Missionary societies, particularly in the Lower River area, constantly found themselves wrong-footed, with resources of staff and buildings in the wrong place. People were on the move from villages into towns, especially to what was to become the sprawling metropolis of Leopold-ville, formerly (and later) Kinshasa.

As missionaries struggled to keep up with the changes and grasp the opportunities, they saw all too clearly the social cost of such rapid change. The first West Central Africa Missionary Conference after the war met in Leopoldville, now the administrative centre of the BMS as well as of the government. In the streets dominated by the

Lever Bros. factory, thousands of children roamed idly
with no hope of a place at school. Feuds broke out between
people of different tribes, though Lingala was becoming a
common language. The Baptist church in the main African
area of the town held two Sunday morning services, one in
Lingala, one in Kikongo. It was a tacit acceptance of the
continuing tribal barriers that would make independence,
when it came, so difficult.

At the Conference, missionaries from further up the river
described population movements of a different kind, on to
the plantations of companies which had been granted vast
concessions of land. The staff at Upoto, always a difficult
area of work, gave agonized descriptions of disrupted
family life and of men crowded into settlements without
their wives and children turning to prostitutes or distilling
palm juice to drown their sorrows.

Yet, for the BMS, the years of war that had been the
trigger for such turmoil had been brightened by the 150th
birthday celebration in 1942. Money from the Ter-Jubilee
fund had been earmarked to meet the desperate need for
training institutes for pastors and teachers at Kibokolo in
Angola and at Yalemba in Upper Congo. The appeal had
also been, however, for 150 new offers of service to the
BMS. Amongst those who came forward in 1942 was a
seventeen-year-old girl, Eileen and her friend, Peter, who
was just fifteen. In the face of such determined young faith,
the Society told Eileen to train as a nurse and Peter to train as
a teacher. In 1953 Peter and Eileen Briggs arrived at Yalikina
at the mouth of the river Lomami in Upper Congo to take
charge of the dispensary and a large regional school of
nearly a thousand pupils.

If in Belgian Congo both government and mission were
struggling to keep up with social change, at least they were
now trying to do so in co-operation. Not so in Portuguese
Congo. Angola had had a different war. Portugal had

remained neutral and the allies had blockaded exports from Angola, so that her economy had stagnated and many young men crossed the border into Belgian Congo.

Relationships between the Portuguese authorities and the BMS, always strained, were tested again when the mission schools at Kibokolo and San Salvador found themselves at the end of the war without the Portuguese heads required under *Decree* 77. With the schools forced to close, the BMS began a desperate search for evangelical Christian teachers from Portugal. The three teachers who finally came, not only to reopen the schools on the stations but to establish a network of village schools, included Avelino Ferreira, who was to give forty years of his life to the work of the BMS, first in Angola and later in Brazil.

But it was very difficult to maintain either education or church life in the rural areas, for the Portuguese authorities were using the population as contract labour. Church buildings stood empty in neglected villages, as the men were forced to work long hours for little or no pay on the rubber plantations or in the copper mines. Meanwhile the women were effectively driven from their homes to grow peanuts and beans in large 'gardens' so far from their villages that they had to live in makeshift huts. Even the children were more often forced to work on the roads than allowed to be in school.

Care of the churches became almost impossible for the young African pastors. The missionaries, angry at the injustices, found themselves once more at odds with the state. And amongst the ordinary Angolan people were being sewn the seeds of a resentment that would one day tear the country apart.

*

'Which of you, if a friend comes asking for bread at night,

will not get up and give it to him?' Perhaps, at four o'clock one Bolobo morning, the staff of the mission hospital remembered the words of Jesus as a commotion outside announced the arrival of one more person needing help.

The disturbed night had followed an exasperating day. Elsewhere in Belgian Congo in the 1950s, state medical provision was steadily growing. But here, in the still remote area of river and forest, the mission hospital remained the only medical centre, apart from village dispensaries, within a radius of 100 miles. The hospital, which treated 3,500 patients each year, was tonight packed to overflowing, with patients and their helpers asleep on the floors. During the day tempers had flared as patients had spilled over also into consulting rooms and laboratories. And now, towards the end of a night in which there had been little rest for anyone in the teeming buildings, here was a young man saying that he had brought his wife in to have her baby. Wearily the nurses went to look at the young woman. She was sixteen years old, in labour with her first child. She had come a hundred miles, sitting on her husband's bicycle, pushed by him all the way. How could they not, somehow, find room for her?

For all the practical problems of space and resources, it was a welcome sign of changed times. Until recently, many women in complicated labour had remained in agony in the 'care' of the grandmothers of the village; twins, regarded as unlucky, had been left to die; the superstitions of the tribes in the Yakusu area had made it impossible for the doctors there to perform Caesarian sections; but now, in all the BMS hospitals antenatal care and obstetrics were saving the lives of both mothers and babies. And the Gospel was being preached. As the newest arrival was delivered in the Bolobo hospital early that morning, the African hospital evangelist was leading prayers in the already bustling outpatients department. He knew that the Bible story he would tell in the wards that day would be passed on next week in the home villages of discharged patients.

Staffing and equipping five hospitals in Congo was a heavy drain on BMS resources. When the missionaries withdrew from China, one of them, Dr S. L. Henderson Smith found himself desperately needed at Pimu, where work had been restricted for lack of a doctor. Yet when the BMS was asked to share in a remarkable venture of co-operation with four other societies at Kimpese, they knew they could not refuse.

L'Institut Medical Evangelique (IME), opened in June 1953, brought together American Baptists, Swedish Con-gregationalists, the Disciples of Christ Congo Mission, the Christian Missionary Alliance and the BMS, who provided Dr Ernest Price. IME was a general hospital with a medical school, but Dr Price was particularly interested in ortho-paedics. Before long the Institute had a seventy-five-bed orthopaedic unit and a workshop that was to provide the first artificial limbs made in Congo.

To the hospital at Kimpese came hundreds of young men crippled as the result of polio in childhood or with amputations following accidents. Ernest Price was to prove that the power to make the lame walk was as real in twentieth-century Congo as it had been in first-century Palestine. It was, however, a rather slower process, and it needed the healing skills of more than just one man, as the doctor himself was the first to point out:

'The patients are mostly old infantile-paralysis cases, who through lack of proper care often arrive with crippling contractures. As a result of their inability to walk, they have often spent their whole lives in a dark damp corner of a village hut; their minds have become as warped from lack of contact with other people as their legs are so obviously bent . . . Often, before treating the deformity or weakness, an attempt has to be made to eradicate malaria, worms, sores and malnutrition. He is gently nursed to fuller health and, should an operation be necessary, the operating and ward staff work together to a common end. Then at the hands of our four devoted young workmen comes the sawing and hammering, soldering, cutting and stitching, until splints and crutches appear from the virgin wood, leather and metal. Following this, the fitting, often with tears, the first halting paces, and finally under the supervision of Matondo, an African assistant who is a trained nurse, the finished result: a confident step with head held high and the scarce-suppressed smile of one who by the grace of God has conquered.'

As in Bolobo the hospital staff acted out the parable of the available friend and in Kimpese the lame were being made to walk, at Yalisombo near Yakusu they were recalling the story of the Grateful Samaritan. In a stifling chapel of burnt brick with a corrugated iron roof, crowded with hundreds of excited people, restless children, babies being nursed by their mothers, the story of the man who gave thanks to Jesus for healing his skin disease was coming alive, Congo-style. It was coming alive for dozens of people who ten years ago had had no hope of a cure for their leprosy but who today were well. It was coming alive for the infirmiers who had been able to witness the first cures of lepromatous leprosy in Central Africa and who today were to sing the Hallelujah Chorus. It was coming alive for Dr Stanley Browne who had arrived in Yakusu in 1936 after training at King's College Hospital and at the School of Tropical Medicine in Antwerp, one of many extraordinarily gifted men who put the claims of Christian mission before the possibilities of financial and professional reward.

The 'Grateful Samaritan' services, after which cured patients were discharged from the leprosarium across the river from Yakusu, never lost their power to move. For Yalisombo had not always been a place of hope and gratitude. In the 1940s, when the Belgian authorities had urged the Yakusu doctors to take on the scourge of leprosy as they had taken on and eradicated sleeping sickness, leprosy sufferers persuaded to come to Yalisombo had seen no reason to stay.

They disliked living amongst people of other tribes. They hated the painful injections of chaulmoogra oil, the only known treatment but one lacking any signs of real success except in very early and mild cases. Their suspicions that the doctors were failing had been confirmed on the day that Dickie Likoso, known to be one of the most brilliant infirmiers ever trained at Yakusu, was himself rowed across the river in stunned silence, tell-tale patches on his skin. 'Why stay?' the leprosy sufferers had asked themselves. They hadn't.

They had been discouraging years. It would have been easy to give up the battle, for there was plenty of other work for the doctors to do. One event, one memory, had revived Stanley Browne's determination each time it had begun to flag. In his early years at Yakusu, he had seen many people around the hospitals with early symptoms of leprosy. He knew that it was a disease that ultimately deformed and crippled its victims. But where were the people with 'the bad leprosy'? Why did he not see any in Yakusu?

One day, on a medical itineration, Stanley Browne had found the answer to his question. Hidden away in the depths of the forest, he had stumbled upon a group of starving creatures, covered with the ulcers of leprosy, blinded, crawling on the stumps of limbs. They had been driven out of society by that most ancient dreaded disease. That memory of what leprosy could do kept him determined to fight it. But with what?

The answer had come in the late 1940s in the form of some drug samples sent to Yakusu for clinical trial by the American Mission to Lepers. The drug was diasone, a derivative of dapsone. The accompanying literature had warned of side-effects that a potential 'guinea-pig' would have to accept. Across the river, his life's work in ruins, was Dickie, his disease progressing relentlessly. Dickie had what was needed in a volunteer to test the drug: he had medical knowledge himself; he had courage; he had Christian faith.

His fellow sufferers at Yalisombo had watched Dickie as he took the new drug and waited. The patches on his skin had begun to regain their pigment. His thickened ears were returning to normal. The word was that smears under the microscope were showing fewer traces of leprosy bacilli. The treatment had worked. In two years the population at Yalisombo rocketed from 118 to 1025, and the drug came into use at Pimu and Ntondo. Many of the patients pronounced free to go home first professed not only gratitude, but Christian faith in baptism.

As in the rapidly growing churches (Bolobo church members were again being disciplined), 'success' brought its problems. The glare of the international spotlight on Yakusu created tensions amongst staff, while other stations were concerned about the equitable distribution of resources. Despite the tensions, the medical work at Yakusu flourished. Stanley Browne left the BMS in 1959 but continued worldwide the fight against leprosy that he had begun in Congo.

*

There were now nearly 50,000 Baptist church members in Congo and Angola. Fully occupied with work in hospitals, schools and churches it was not surprising if BMS staff in Belgian Congo in the mid-1950s saw the devolution of power to the Congolese churches as something that would happen, probably gradually, 'one day', rather than as something requiring urgent attention.

They were uneasily aware of the re-emergence of Kimbanguism, a 'prophet movement' focused on Simon Kimbangu, an influential member of the Wathen Church in the 1920s, whose adherents had been forced underground by the Belgian authorities. At times some of the able young Christians who had come through the schools and training institutes sought out the missionaries in attempts to clarify their own responses to new ideas of nationalism. Mission staff were also aware that the first Congolese political party founded in Leopoldville in 1956 had as one of its leaders a deacon from the Baptist Church of S. Jean in the suburbs of the city. Though apolitical themselves, the missionaries sensed that it was perhaps inevitable that young Christians should be drawn into the political arena. In fact, every one of the African nations that achieved independence in the post-war era was led by a man who had been educated by missionaries.

The background of heightened political awareness nagged at the missionary consciousness, mainly because they suspected that it would make their preaching, teaching and medical work more difficult. What they did not envisage was that within five years events would turn Congo upside down and force, not gradually but suddenly, the integration of mission and Congolese church.

Ghana gained independence in 1957. The following year, Congolese representatives attended an All-Africa People's Conference at Accra. On their return to Congo, attempts to prevent their speaking at a meeting sparked off riots in Leopoldville. As the whole of Congo seethed with the determination to be free of colonial rule, the Belgian King promised to grant independence on 30th June 1960.

The euphoria of Independence Day was short-lived. Congolese troops at Leopoldville and Thysville mutinied against their white officers. Fighting broke out between

Belgian and African troops. More out of fear of rumoured
Russian invasion than of fear of the African people, some
BMS missionaries were briefly evacuated from Lower and
Upper Congo. With calm restored by United Nations
troops, it was possible in August for a BMS delegation of
Ernest Madge, Overseas Secretary of the Society, and its
Vice-Chairman, Professor H. Rowley, to visit Congo. The
devolution of control of the mission's work to the churches
was now imperative.

BMS staff were in no doubt that they were still greatly
needed, especially after the exodus of many foreign doctors
during the period of unrest. The infirmiers were proving
their worth in medical care, and, as the education of leaders
for both church and state were clearly vital, two new
secondary schools were established in 1960, one at Ngombe
Lutete and one at Bolobo. But, needed as the missionaries
were and would be for years to come, their relationship to
their people had changed. The paternalism of less than a
hundred years before belonged to a very different age. On
1st January 1961, BMS staff in the Republic of Congo
became members of, and answerable to, one of three Baptist
Churches – of the Lower River, the Middle River or of
Upper Congo.

No sooner was a degree of stability regained in Congo
than all the resentment at forced labour and the harshness of
Portuguese rule erupted in Angola. For some time, would-
be political activists, denied the rights to form political
parties in Angola, had crossed into Congo and there formed
the Union of the Peoples of Angola. At the instigation of the
UPA riots broke out in Northern Angola in March 1961,
and hundreds of Portuguese were killed. The Portuguese
community responded and the army moved in to massacre
tens of thousands of civilians, lay waste their villages,
destroy the mission station at Bembe and commandeer the
San Salvador site for a garrison. It seemed to the mission

staff, airlifted temporarily to Luanda as their congregations fled in terror through the forest and across the border into Congo, that nearly a century of work was falling about their ears.

Two new tasks now lay before the BMS. One was to follow the refugees into the Lower River area of Congo, where the hospital at Kimpese was overflowing with sick and wounded refugees and where by the end of the year there were 58,000 Angolans at Kibentele in need of food and shelter. The other was to make known in England the truth not only about the horrors currently being unleashed on the African people but about the decades of Portuguese brutality that had preceded them.

For Baptists with a sense of history, the campaign of conscience triggered in England by an address by former Angolan missionary, Clifford Parsons, to the Baptist Assembly held echoes of that waged by William Knibb. Stories of the atrocities in Angola were taken up by the media and laid before the MacMillan government. On one Sunday, a petition urging action to stop the bloodshed by the Portuguese received over 35,000 signatures in British churches. Concern aroused in the international community brought the issues before the World Council of Churches and the United Nations.

Yet the story in Angola continued. By the end of 1964 nearly half a million Angolans had fled into the Lower River region of Congo, where missionaries under David Grenfell struggled to feed, teach and heal them and to encourage the Baptists amongst them to find a spiritual home, at least for the time being, in the Church of the Lower River.

9. Mission on the Move

Brazil 1953 to 1991

The BMS had received a 'Macedonian call'. It had come, in the perhaps unlikely setting of a conference lunch queue, to Kathleen and Arthur Elder.

Forced out of China in the early 1950s, the BMS had been asked to consider the possibility of working in South America. Their response had been to send the Elders to Brazil on an 'information gathering exercise'. So it was that Kathleen and Arthur had found themselves at a conference of the Youth Department of the Baptist World Alliance in the city of Rio de Janeiro.

Their neighbour in the queue, to whom the Elders explained that, now that they could no longer work in China, they were waiting to know what God wanted them to do, was a Baptist minister from the south of Brazil. His response was 'Come to Parana and help us'. It was as unequivocal and directly personal a request as that in Paul's dream in Acts 16.

Why Parana? In the early 1950s, people were moving from all over the vast country of Brazil, fourth largest in the world but still largely unexplored, into the state of Parana. It was the start of a movement that would send the population of Parana soaring by five million in two decades. They came – people from the drought-stricken areas of North-East Brazil, people from beautiful but overcrowded Rio, trapped between the mountains and the sea, people from Sao Paulo, a 'coffee capital' whose coffee groves were becoming exhausted. They came in the hope of a new life, and their hopes had a firmer foundation than was often the case. An English-based company had bought up tracts of the Parana pine forest from the Brazilian government and was offering strips of land for sale – genuine documents for hard cash – to those who would farm and live there. There were to be no absentee landlords. So, as the Elders listened over lunch in Rio to their first stories of Parana, young couples with their small children were streaming into north-west Parana. They were beginning to clear the beautiful pine trees, to plant coffee to sell and maize, rice and beans to live on. Some of these people on the move were Christians.

Because of its colonization by Portugal, Brazil was predominantly, though often nominally, a Roman Catholic country. The Brazilian Roman Catholic church in the 1950s was a far cry from the renewed church of today. In the face of great poverty, its hierarchy was unashamedly wealthy; its priesthood frequently corrupt; its people trapped in an ignorance and superstition that often owed more to African voodoo and spiritism than to the Gospel of Jesus Christ.

Missionaries from the Southern Baptist Convention of the United States had been working in Brazil since the end of the nineteenth century. It was not surprising, in the light of Brazilian Catholicism, that they were establishing churches of a very evangelistic character, with great emphasis on the importance of Scripture and with such an abhorrence of Roman Catholicism that no Baptist building would display even an unadorned wooden cross.

Many of the families who were now building their little wooden houses alongside the Parana dirt roads that were red dust in summer and thick mud in winter had come from areas where Southern Baptist missionaries had been working. It was natural for those who maintained that 'every Baptist home is a preaching station' to invite in their neighbours and to begin to talk about their faith. They could not have had a more receptive climate in which to do so. They were speaking to people in all the excitement of a new life, open to new ideas. They were alongside people experiencing the tragedies that inevitably marked a pioneer situation – tragedies that soon brought rows of tiny graves outside the new towns – and who needed Christian comfort and Christian testimony.

Soon small gatherings in overcrowded living rooms became infant congregations, eager to worship, wanting to learn. What they needed, and needed urgently, were pastors. Preferably on wheels. Preferably wheels with four-wheel drive! The Parana Baptist Convention was based in the elegant city of Curitiba, where there was a strong church in the city centre, smaller churches in the suburbs and a church at the port of Paranagua on the coast. But Curitiba with its small Bible Institute was hundreds of dirt-track miles away from north west Parana. The Convention could not hope to supply the growing and insistent need for pastoral oversight in 'the interior'. So had come that Macedonian call: 'Come to Parana and help us.'

Arthur Elder had been born in South America, the son of missionaries in Argentina. He and Kathleen had no doubt that the Lord was speaking to them. Could they now convince the BMS, forced out of China, that Brazil and more specifically Parana was to be its new 'field'?

There were some who needed little convincing. Some, including Victor Hayward who had come home from China to become Secretary of the BMS, were ready not just for a new 'field', as it was still described, but for a new missionary strategy. They were ready for a way of working that would refuse to become entrapped in mission stations and institutions. The schools, colleges and hospitals established with the best of motives by the Society in India, Africa and China, now appeared to many people to have circumscribed its work. They had pinned down staff on one station for decades, failing to take account of the fact that populations move, just as people were now on the move in Brazil. Like other missionary societies, the BMS had at times been wrong-footed, left with expensive buildings and personnel in the wrong place when the people they had come to serve moved on. Now there were other problems. With the withdrawal of the BMS from China and the establishing of independent churches in India, those institutions were likely to prove not just a legacy but a burden to young indigenous churches. So there were those who, having learned some lessons, were eager now to try a new way of working. Brazil seemed to offer just that – an opportunity for mobile and flexible evangelism within a church that would from the start be self-governing, self-supporting and self-propagating.

The BMS was not alone in scrutinizing the style and strategy of its mission over a century and a half. Other denominations and societies were treading the same path. In *One Body, One Gospel, One World*, Bishop Lesslie Newbigin wrote:

> The modern missionary movement has not been successful in following the example of St Paul, who could leave behind a living church at the end of a few months or years of work and move on to a new region. The profound theological reasons for this failure have been brilliantly analysed by Roland Allen in his well-known books . . . By far the greater number of foreign missionaries in the past two centuries have been those who spent their lives in one area, perhaps one station, building up one institution or one group of churches . . . To have an institution or a station manned by generation after generation of missionaries, and to be told after a century or two that it is still urgently necessary to send a new missionary to fill the vacancy caused by the retirement of

the last one may be traditional in modern missions, but it is something very remote from the missionary methods of St Paul.

Into this climate of debate, this readiness to change both the assumptions and methods of mission, had come the 'Macedonian call'. But there were those who, for very good reasons, argued strongly against the BMS putting resources of personnel and money into another continent.

Look at the unmet needs and unexploited opportunities they pointed out, in the countries where the Society was already working. Look at overstretched pastors, at under-staffed hospitals. Look particularly at Angola – at the suffering of the people there and their need for education and for medical and pastoral care. The BMS already had a commitment to the Angolan people. If there were money and staff available, they were needed there.

A Macedonian call? Or a diversion from existing responsibilities? They were not easy claims to resolve. The short-term solution was to give Kathleen and Arthur Elder two years to assess and report back on the possibilities of work in Parana.

As Arthur and Kathleen were aware, there could have been no greater contrast than that of China and Brazil. For just under a century, the missionaries in China had struggled to cross almost closed frontiers. The cultural and spiritual doors of China had never been more than slightly ajar. But Brazil, as people of all nationalities were discovering, was a country of open doors. Since the start of the twentieth century, and especially since World War II, European refugees, from Germany, Poland and Italy, had settled in the most southerly states of Brazil, building European-style houses and retaining their own language alongside Portuguese. Meanwhile Japanese had come to start a new life in the state of Sao Paulo. The vast uncharted areas of Brazil lured explorers, while engineers and technicians found their skills more than welcome in a fast-developing country. For the young and for those who for whatever reason wanted to start again, for the gifted and the courageous – and now perhaps for the BMS – Brazil had an open door of opportunity.

*

The jeep had been bumping along the track, past coffee groves, over the Picquiri ferry and through the forest for nine hours. Nine hours since Derek Winter with a small group of Christians from the church at Clanorte had left home to come to help Cecilio. But suddenly, as the jeep swung off the dirt road into a clearing in the forest, there, caught in its headlights was Cecilio, his dark lean face lit up by a huge smile of welcome, his arms open already to hug his friends as they spilled out of the jeep for an exuberant Brazilian embrace.

Weary as the travellers were, there was no question of sleep yet in the little hut, five metres square, its walls of split palm trunk, its roof slats of cedar, that was Cecilio's new home. It was time for strong black coffee in the dancing light of the paraffin lamp, and time to catch up on the news. Good news. The visitors from Cianorte could hardly wait to tell Cecilio how the church there, which had started with just two families, meeting first in a home and then in a rented hall, was growing. Every week there were new faces at the Bible Study, little ones toddling happily around and babies dozing on their mothers' laps, for, when Brazilians went out, they went as a family.

They missed Cecilio in the Cianorte church, but they understood why he had moved out to his own strip of jungle in the fertile Picquiri Valley to plant coffee. They knew that he had come also to sow the seeds of the Gospel.

Now Cecilio's friends had made their nine-hour trip to help him to build a chapel in the little village of Caraja, a mile from his home.

Eventually they slept. The next few days were to prove a tantalizing mixture of frustration and furious activity. The local sawmill failed to deliver the timber promised for the chapel building; they had sold it to someone else instead. But the little group of Christians could, if they liked, take what they could find in the timber yard for the floor and walls. The jungle itself was scoured for suitable slats for the roofs, for tiles were too expensive.

By Sunday, the building was up, open for a service of thanksgiving and dedication. It was the first place of worship in Caraja and would be the venue each Sunday morning for the all-age Sunday School that was a feature both of Southern Baptist and of Brazilian church life. In the morning, Bible study and teaching; in the evening, the evangelistic address and the appeal for people to commit their lives to Christ.

It was hard for the visitors to tear themselves away. As one or other went back for a last tearful hug of farewell, Derek started the jeep's engine and looked at the sign that Cecilio had placed at the entrance to his farm. Since he himself was Cecilio de Oliveira, he had called it 'Olive Tree Farm', and under the name was a text from the Old Testament prophet Zachariah about olive trees. The text ended with the words, 'Not by might, nor by power, but by my spirit, says the Lord.'

As the jeep bumped back towards Cianorte, Derek's passengers talking excitedly, he was turning over in his mind the words he had just read. He knew that it was by the Holy Spirit that Arthur Elder's compelling report to the BMS had paved the way for him and his wife, Beryl, to come to Parana as the second missionary couple. He knew that it was by the Holy Spirit that the church at Cianorte was growing from two families to 500 members, meeting in several congregations throughout the town, in six years. It was by the Holy Spirit that the British missionaries were being enabled to help the Brazilian Christians who, as Cecilio himself had demonstrated, were themselves the evangelists.

Back across the Picquiri River, back through areas where the forest had been cleared and burned and the coffee planted, Derek knew that he would soon be on the road again. A new congregation was being formed sixty miles west of Cianorte at a little town that went by the lovely name of Umuarama, 'the place where friends meet'. If Victor Hayward and others had had a vision of mobile evangelism, then this was surely it.

'It is part of the missionary's job,' Derek was to write home, 'to be constantly on the move, visiting outlying congregations and preaching points, putting one small group of believers in touch with another, helping isolated Christians to feel that they belong to a wider fellowship which knows about them and cares for them. He must do the work of an evangelist, backing up the missionary outreach of the people themselves . . . and he must be teacher and pastor, helping to sort out the problems which so often arise in young and inexperienced churches and . . . helping to train leaders.'

*

William Carey – and many successive missionaries to India – had picked up as much Bengali as possible from John Thomas on board ship. Timothy Richard had grappled with the 214 Chinese radicals somewhere between Hong Kong and Shanghai. Later, as language training became more formal, Isabel Angus had had to pass exams in Urdu, and new missionaries bound for Congo had received language training in Belgium.

The missionary couples arriving in Brazil – the Elders and Winters were followed in 1959 by the Brunton Scotts – might have found studying Brazilian Portuguese at an American language school at Campinas something of a luxury had it not been for a sense of urgency to complete the course as fast as possible.

Thirty families a day were arriving in Cianorte. Many had never heard the Gospel, never handled a Bible. Yet all across northern Parana, new Christians were erecting places for worship. Except for the building in the town of Cascavel, so strategically sited that the Parana Convention felt it must fund a building there, their meeting places were financed by the people themselves. They were willingly adopting the Southern Baptist emphasis on tithing – the giving of a tenth of their income, sometimes as money, sometimes in the form of timber or other building materials, to the church. Not for them the closely-guarded secrets of personal income and anonymous offering envelopes of British Baptists. Every Brazilian church member knew what his brother earned and what he gave – and was ready to call him to account in church meeting if one did not relate to the other.

The churches tithed, too, for the work of the state convention and for the national and overseas missions. In his 1956 report, Arthur Elder had ventured to tell the BMS that 'Some even speak of Brazil as the great missionary-sending country of the future.' Already the tithes of Parana immigrants, bringing up their children on their strips of land with rice, beans and chicken, were supporting Brazilian missionaries in Bolivia. By 1990, one hundred and six Brazilian Baptist missionaries would be working in eighteen countries of the world.

Spurred on by this enthusiasm in the Brazilian Christians, the three BMS couples and the Convention appealed for more help. The Society's response was to send five more couples between 1960 and 1965: the Dellers, the Clarkes, the Doonans and, relocated from Angola, the Boornes and the Ferreiras. As pioneer evangelism and church planting continued, with churches being handed over to Brazilian pastors as soon as they could support them, the missionaries were turning their eyes to wider horizons. Arthur Elder, who had become Secretary of the Convention and was teaching in the Bible Institute in Curitiba, spoke for them all when he urged the BMS to consider expansion, both in the type and geographical location of its work. The churches needed pastors. The Curitiba Bible Institute was able to do no more than prepare a few young men from the state each year for further training in one of the seminaries in Rio or Recife. Could not the Institute, with BMS help, be upgraded to a seminary? Was it not time for the BMS itself to become involved in theological education?

The Society had a dilemma. Its initial commitment to work in Brazil, in the face of Arthur Elder's challenge that 'When there is evident movement of God's spirit in a nation, we should do all we can to help and guide that movement', had been limited. Now, in 1964, the Angolan refugees in Lower Congo numbered nearly half a million and they were desperate for help. Expansion in Brazil? The Society's next move, as so often over the centuries, was to send two of its officers to see for themselves. The two Secretaries, Ernest Madge and Alberic Clement, visited Brazil in June 1965. Their report gave the green light, or at any rate an amber one, for a degree of BMS involvement in theological education, providing that the main thrust of its work remained in church planting.

Yet there were other pressing concerns. All the missionaries were painfully aware that they were able to visit remote congregations only once every three months. On those occasions, they would baptize the new converts. But what happened after that? Who, in those scattered congregations, had the skills and spiritual maturity to care for and teach the young Christians?

David and Doris Doonan had arrived in Brazil in 1964 and begun work at Umuarama, now a church of 350 with seven congregations. The following year Avelino and Ana Ferreira had settled in the old town of Jacarezinho in the north of the state. The Irishman and the little Portuguese with the big personality soon discovered what they shared – an impatience to get on with training lay leadership within the churches.

It was not going to be easy. They would have to sell the idea carefully to the Brazilian pastors who, while professing 'the priesthood of all believers' were not too sure about its practice. They themselves had made great sacrifices in order to be trained and ordained and it was not easy for them to accept the idea of lay people having responsibility in the churches.

Nor was the teaching itself going to be easy, though Avelino had taught in Angola. Brazilian state education was in its infancy and had come too late for the coffee farmers and bricklayers of the Parana churches. As David looked at the twenty-five fathers and grandfathers who gathered in the Cianorte church in December 1967 for the first 'extension course', he knew that many of them had learned to read only when they became Christians and wanted to read the Bible for themselves.

Could they do it? Could they cope with these manuals for Church Organization and Sunday School teaching, prepared by the Baptist publishing house in Rio? What would happen at the end of the two week course, when they went home to study night after night after a full day's work? Would they send in their work for marking? Would they take time off work again in six months to come back for exams and further study? Could they sustain this for three years?

David found a desperate-looking member of the course with his head under a cold tap.

'Pastor, my head is boiling!' he explained. He had never sat at a desk before in his life. Now here he was, studying the Old Testament and Church History.

Yet before long the evidence of a less superficial teaching and fewer spiritual crises in the churches was clear. Before long, too, the pattern of extension work was taken up, on the beautiful but remote coastal strip of the Litoral by John Clark, and in the mushrooming town of Londrina by American Bill Smith, backed up British missionary Derek Punchard.

As the patient training of the many continued, so BMS involvement in the setting apart of the few gathered pace. Derek Winter and later David Doonan joined the staff of the Bible Institute in Curitiba, which became a seminary in 1974. Tony Boorne was seconded to the staff of the Recife seminary. Yet fully involved as the missionaries were in the churches and in their training of their leaders, their eyes went again and again beyond Parana.

When in 1965 the BMS had said 'Yes' to theological education, they had said 'No' to geographical expansion. Yet patterns of life for the Brazilian people were, by the late 60s, changing again. The rate of migration into Parana had slowed and many of those families that did arrive found the area too expensive and carried on their journey, across the river Parana, into the southern areas of the vast state of Mato Grosso. Meanwhile the small farmers of the 50s were being bought out by large landowners, anxious to replace the coffee groves with cattle ranches and soya plantations. Too late, the people found that mechanization brought redundancy and the drift to the cities of Curitiba and the neighbouring state capital of Sao Paulo.

By 1970, when the Brazilian economy was booming with the investment of foreign capital and technology, the

Brazilian people were on the move again, this time north and west into the undeveloped regions and untapped possibilities of Amazonas, Rondonia and northern Mato Grosso. They went as they had gone before, in search of some often elusive dream of a better life for themselves and their children. As the missionaries watched, aware that what they were charged with was the consolidation of their work in Parana, many of them longed to follow.

★

The new missionary in the city of Sao Paulo, struggling to adjust not only to the language but also to the culture of Brazil, tried to explain her feelings to her Brazilian language teacher.

'I think,' she said, 'that it will take me a little while to settle down.'

The teacher looked at her in bewilderment. There was, the missionary discovered, no word in Brazilian Portuguese for 'settle down'.

How can there be a word for 'settle down' in Sao Paulo, third largest city in the world, largest in the southern hemisphere, commercial centre of Brazil? Day and night, the cars never stop streaming round its orbital road, so that pollution hangs over the city like a wreath and grounds its planes. Day and night, the people – of every racial origin and shade of skin – never stop streaming through its streets, over its bridges, down into its metro system.

To be rich in Sao Paulo is to live higher and higher off the ground, for high-rise apartments, protected by armed guards, are safer than houses. To be poor in Sao Paulo is to gather together a shelter for yourself and your children on the edge of a favela, first from hardboard and scraps of timber, then with a few bricks. You never forget that you are poor, for the rich are just around the corner.

To be young in Sao Paulo is often to be abandoned by parents who have moved on; to live with other homeless children – one million street children in this one city – near the Cathedral, curtained by palm trees, and to wash youself in its elegant fountains. To live by your wits, by begging, car-cleaning, theft, prostitution, and then perhaps, picked out by a local shopkeeper – 'that one' – as a nuisance, to be quietly shot by police to keep the streets 'clean'.

How can there be a word for 'settle down' in Sao Paulo, where rich, poor, young are always on the move? Yet here, in 1974, the BMS in an attempt to solve the age-old problem of the education of missionaries' children, opened a hostel so that children between the ages of nine and sixteen could go to the English-speaking school of St Paul's.

The succession of couples who came to take on the difficult rôle of 'hostel parents' and those missionaries who later came to establish an administrative centre for the Society's work were confronted day by day with the yawning chasm of injustice that separated the sophisticated Paulistas of the business centre from the misery of the families of the favelas. So here today a young missionary couple has been designated specifically for urban mission, working in the sprawling industrial area of Sao Bernardo in favelas from which the children do not emerge to go to school and into which no doctor will venture.

How can there be a word for 'settle down' in Rio de Janeiro, city of samba and carnival and street violence?

'They tell me', says an elderly woman in a little Baptist church, 'that Rio is a beautiful city. I can't see it myself.' The Rio she knows is not the Rio of the filmstar luxury of Copacabana Beach or the Rio of the stunning natural beauty of the Sugarloaf Mountain towering over the bay, but the Rio of the littered street markets and the favelas.

How can you settle down even in a favela in Rio, when the shelters are built one on top of another like a precarious house of cards clinging to the mountainside, to be washed away when the rains come? Yet here in 1990 a British Baptist missionary works with the overseas mission board of the Brazilian Baptist Convention. And here in a little bullet-marked favela church, built into the side of the mountain on four floors, the Christians run classes in sewing and typing to help local mothers earn a little money working at home. Here the Christians, Bibles under their arms, used to be able to walk respected and unmolested through the narrow alleyways and open sewers of the favela. That was before the police, dressed as Baptists and with Bibles under their arms, entered the favela to raid it for drugs.

Even away from the cities, how can there be a word for 'settle down' amongst people who find that, having cleared and burnt the rainforest to plant crops, the soil thus exploited is exhausted in a couple of years so that they have to move on and slash and burn again in order to support their families?

Yet today, on the litoral of Parana, a Baptist agricultural missionary, in a project sponsored by the Baptist Convention, demonstrates how to farm without destroying the forest and abusing the land; how to contour the land so that soil is not eroded and crops not washed away by rains; how to plant fast-growing trees that shelter the crops and restore the soil. Today he teaches the small children of the scattered communities, tomorrow's farmers, to tend their little vegetable gardens.

And today, along the still mud road that weaves along the coast, a request for help comes to the 'Good Samaritan' dispensary at Tagacaba. The sixteen-year-old wife of a farmhand is ill. She was sent home from hospital thirty miles away, two days after the Caesarian delivery of her second baby, and now she has a cough and a pain in her chest. Will the Brazilian Baptist nurse, who divides her time between preaching and healing, come?

There is no word in Brazilian Portuguese for 'settle down'.

And there is no true outworking of the Gospel that takes no account of poverty and injustice. By 1974 the BMS had had no choice but to move on.

*

In the breathtaking economic boom of the early 70s, when for the wealthy and able anything seemed possible, though for the poorest drifting into the cities mere survival became a challenge, great new highways were driven deep into the interior of Brazil. They opened up the way to clear the forest for ranching and agriculture and to prospect for minerals, including gold. The three-hundred-year-old capital of the vast state of Mato Grosso, Cuiaba, situated at the very heart of South America, became accessible by a new road for the first time from the south of Brazil. Further north the road pushed on into the territory of Rondonia. Its capital, Porto Velho, had been born in the days when rubber was the main product of Brazil, and was now on the verge of a rebirth.

In February 1972, on a visit to the Amazonas Baptist Convention, Roy Deller, experienced in church planting and as Convention Secretary in Parana, saw the new highways and was caught up in all the expectancy and excitement of what they meant.

'To me,' he reported back to his colleagues and to the BMS, 'the challenge is obvious and also the opportunity. It is the road and the inevitable attraction to the naturally migrant Brazilian land worker.'

Although in 1972 it was primarily in terms of Rondonia and especially of Porto Velho that Roy Deller saw 'the challenge and the opportunity', it was in fact into Mato Grosso that the BMS made its first geographical move beyond Parana. It was, after all, across the river Parana and into Mato Grosso that both missionaries and people had been looking wonderingly for a decade.

The huge state stretched north across flat land being burnt and cleared so fast for soya and cattle that the great empty horizons were still broken by the charred stumps of trees. It stretched west across the rivers and marshes of the Pantanal, home of exotic wildlife and of scattered Indian tribes, to the Bolivian border. It stretched north through still dense rainforest to the rim of the Amazon basin. It held all the variety and potential that makes Brazil itself such an indefinable country.

The first movements of missionaries were into the north of the state – David and Eileen MacClenaghan to Cuiaba, followed by Peter and Susan Cousins, who, as new towns sprung up across the north, moved on to Arenapolis and Sinop. Stuart and Georgie Christine saw the town of Jaciara grow from 14,000 to 20,000 during the two years that they cared for five mission points there. In 1979, as people poured into Mato Grosso, the state was divided, two thirds of it remaining Mato Grosso and the most southerly third becoming Mato Grosso do Sol.

People were coming, churches were growing, Baptists were tithing, generous to each other's congregations and, like New Testament Christians, willing even to send money to churches they would never see thousands of miles away on the borders with Paraguay. Yet it was not like the heady years of Parana all over again.

This was a new generation of migrants and many of them had come from Parana. It was not the first time they had opened a Bible for themselves. It was not the first time that they or someone close to them had been exposed to the Gospel.

'Baptist? Oh, yes,' the new arrivals would tell a missionary or Brazilian pastor pleasantly, 'my parents used to be Baptists in Parana.' Or even, since Brazilian Baptist practice was to baptize youngsters who had made a

Christian commitment at what was by British standards an early age: 'Oh, yes, I was baptized when I was nine years old in Parana. But that was a long time ago, in my old life.' This time, rather than a spirit of excitement, there was a sense of *déjà vu*. The missionaries in Mato Grosso had a harder task, and less fertile ground in which to sow the seeds of the Gospel, than had their predecessors in Parana.

There was something else to worry the churches of the Centre of America Baptist Convention. Young men from the state were being sent to train for the ministry in the seminaries of Rio and Recife and, allured by a culture that Mato Grosso lacked, were failing to return.

*

The city of Cuiaba was growing at the rate of twelve per cent a year. Its old white colonial buildings were dwarfed by new developments. Its outskirts were a sea of mud, bulldozers and pipes, as the city struggled to keep pace with demands for housing, water and electricity. Brazil was borrowing money at a staggering rate, unaware that soaring oil prices would one day plunge the nation into debts it could never repay. Over half the population of Brazil was under sixteen years old, and in the streets of Cuiaba at night small children made their way to school. Elsewhere in Brazil, state education for children of seven and over was organized in three shifts a day to maximise resources of staff and buildings. In Cuiaba, there were four sessions. A city like that surely warranted its own seminary for the state's would-be pastors. It was to the BMS that the Convention looked for a Principal.

In 1980 David Doonan surveyed his seminary 'building'. It was in fact the basement garage of a large house belonging to an American missionary. Later, there would be lean-to buildings in the garden for bathrooms and dormitories, and later, too, David would be joined by Keith Hodges so that extension training as well as ministerial training could be undertaken.

David looked, too, at his students, much younger than the men he had worked with in lay training in Parana, and with some basic education. They were young men and women with all the energy and vitality of the Brazilians, yet they were young men and women under pressure, many of them married with young families to support. In the evening tutorial, Maria's eyes were heavy with tiredness. Although Brazilian Baptist churches did not, and do not, accept women as pastors, Maria was training for three years for leadership in the church. Every morning she worked as a maid to pay her way. Every evening she was here at the seminary, leaving with work to prepare for the next day. In the local church to which she had been assigned, she taught in Sunday School, led a midweek meeting, visited families in the maze of new houses on the edge of the town. There were many Marias. Her tired eyes and her determination to study and to succeed were – and in the Brazil of the 1990s still are – not the exception but the rule.

*

SORRIA. JESUS AMA VOCE. 'Smile. Jesus loves you.' The words are painted in huge letters on the end of a small building in Campo Grande, Mato Grosso do Sol. They are visible across rows of hastily assembled homes in an area of the city 'invaded' by people looking for somewhere to live, somewhere to stop, at any rate for a while. In 1950, at the time of the 'Macedonian call', thirty-eight per cent of the population of Brazil lived in cities. In 1970, at the time of the 'economic miracle', the figure was fifty-six per cent. In 1980, by which time oil prices had soared, commodity prices had tumbled and the shimmering bubble had burst into the largest national debt in the world after that of the USA, sixty-eight per cent of Brazilians lived in cities. Over half of those were children under the age of sixteen.

So, in this area of Campo Grande, where the houses have gone up but without too much else in the way of roads, sewerage, clinics, schools, the local Baptist church has announced that it is nevertheless possible to smile because Jesus loves you, and established a pre-school project for children under seven. Here, in 1990, a little girl frowns with concentration as she handles coloured paper, scissors, pasta shapes and glue. She is making a collage of the numeral that represents her age and beneath her fingers the green, raised, nice-to-touch number 5 is taking shape on a blue background.

It is dark in the small building, but outside in the sunshine the young pastor of the church, black Bible strapped to the back of his bike, stops to talk to a BMS missionary. Frank Gouthwaite has discovered that his work lies in opening the eyes of the Baptist churches of Mato Grosso do Sol to the opportunities not only of preaching and evangelism but of showing practical Christian care within the community.

Across the river Parana, in the town of Nova Londrina, lunchtime is over and the babies are being put into their cots for a sleep. Here the building is larger, lighter, more attractively decorated than in Campo Grande. But perhaps 'Lars Batista' or 'Baptist Home' – 'home' not in the sense of an institution but in the sense of a focal point of love – really means the same as *Sorria. Jesus ama voce*. Here, in 1990, BMS missionary, Gerry Myhill, who built with his own hands the day centre that cares for sixty children from seven in the morning till five in the evening, cuts manioc in the garden which produces food for the children's midday meal.

In Cuiaba in Mato Grosso, a little boy wriggles impatiently on the lap of a worker in a pre-school project sponsored jointly by the Baptist church and an international aid agency. He has already lost the sight of one eye through neglected infection but he hates having drops put into the other. He wants his dinner of blackbeans and rice and then he wants to play outside.

*

Thirty years before the little girl made her collage in Campo Grande, the babies had their afternoon rest in Nova Londrina and the eye drops came out in Cuiaba, Derek Winter wrote that the work that the BMS had been entrusted to do in Brazil had been 'simply the evangelism of the community and the formation of churches which will in their turn serve the community around them.' He was right in foreseeing that much informal service would be offered by Christians who knew what it was in practice to love their neighbour. Despite such spontaneous and informal caring, for two decades two factors militated against any structured 'social activity' by the churches. They were the strongly evangelistic emphasis of the Brazilian Baptists, influenced by American Southern Baptist concern for souls rather than bodies, and the repressive nature of the right-wing military government of Brazil.

But this now is 1990. The military junta has been replaced by a kind of democracy struggling with economic crises which widen the gulf between rich and poor. And the 'inasmuch' of Jesus – inasmuch as you fed me when I was hungry, clothed me when I was naked, visited me when I was sick – will not go away. The Brazilian Baptist church has been set an example in caring for the poor by the two churches of which it is most wary. Brazilian Baptists keep their distance both from Roman Catholics and from Charismatics. Yet it is the base communities of the Roman Catholic church and the Pentecostal Assemblies of God who have shown most readiness to enter the favelas or the suburbs invaded by squatters and to show the wholeness of the Gospel to people there.

Theological, political and social pressures are real. Yet, in 1990, the Brazilian Baptist churches are being challenged to make a more structured response to the needs of their neighbours and especially of the youngest members of the community. The rich in Brazil pay for their education and their health care. For the poor, state education, limited both in quantity and quality, begins at seven years of age. Until they are seven Brazilian children with working mothers sink or swim at home alone or in the care of barely older brothers or sisters. After they are seven, they sink or swim in an educational system in which poorly paid teachers may be on strike for months at a time.

Pre-school provision like that in Campo Grande, in Nova Londrina, in Cuiaba, has many aims. It aims to keep small children safe. It aims to give them one decent meal a day, vital for mental as well as physical development. It aims to give them one shower a day and to explain to mothers that, if they wash the food from round their children's mouths before they go to bed, they are less likely to be bitten by cockroaches. It aims to give them numeracy and literacy skills that will help them make the most of the first couple of years of state education. All these things are part of helping children to smile and to understand that Jesus loves them.

*

But what about Rondonia? What about 'the challenge and the opportunity' that Roy Deller glimpsed in 1972? It was not until 1979 that the BMS was able to respond to an invitation from the Rondonia and Acre Convention and John and Maria Dyer went to Porto Velho. As Roy had foreseen, Porto Velho, almost abandoned with the demise of the rubber trade, had been given a new lease of life with the prospect of gold and of clearing the forest for farmland in the country's fastest growing state.

When the Dyers moved further west along the Madeira River, a tributary of the Amazon, to build up a little church in Rio Negro from fifteen to fifty members, David and Sheila Brown came to Porto Velho. While David began extension training of lay leaders, Sheila, who had been prepared to revalidate her nursing training in Brazil, worked part-time in a health centre and shared in feeding and innoculation programmes for young children. In another move towards multi-ministry, towards caring for people as whole people with minds that need stimulating, bodies that need healing and spirits that need restoring, the Browns set up a forest camp site as a retreat centre for pastors, their wives or for groups of young people.

In 1987 Vince and Sadie MacDougall arrived in Rondonia to train leaders in the church of Cacoal, a strong church with thirteen congregations. The removal of the Browns the following year to Rio de Janeiro, when David was invited to work with the overseas mission board of the national convention, left the MacDougalls as the only BMS staff in Rondonia.

Where will the story of the BMS in Brazil end? Certainly far from where it began. Although the majority of the forty year story has been acted out in Parana, in 1990 only a dozen of the fifty BMS missionaries were working in that state. Others, at the invitation of nine Brazilian Baptist conventions, were scattered the length and breadth of a vast country – from Rondonia in the west to Rio in the east – from the Baptist seminary at Porto Alegre near the border with Uraguay to the hottest, dryest areas of the north east, where two young couples were working, one with the urban poor and one with the rural poor. They respect each other's diversity of vocation and skills. 'I don't know how you can stand the tarantulas and the scorpions,' one young missionary wife says to another. 'I don't know how you can cope with having drug pushers next door,' comes the reply. In the main the BMS missionaries find the fellowship they need not so much with each other as with the Brazilian Christians who are their co-workers in the Gospel. But once a year they do make the journey to meet together, to study, pray, exchange information and relax together. Some of them are bound together by another link, because their children are being cared for in the hostel at Sao Paulo.

In one of the biggest, most violent and most polluted cities in the world, the minibus that has fetched the children from school stops outside the hostel and the children run up the steps. Like all children coming home from school, they want to grumble about their day, they want help with their homework, they want to know what time dinner will be ready. Unlike most children coming home from school, there is no opportunity for them to go out again to play with friends or to walk to a park. They have to find both family life and friendship within the hostel.

John and Maria Dyer, latest in a long line of hostel parents, have discovered what it is to be missionaries in a country where people are always on the move. They have worked in churches deep in the forested areas of the north west. They have led extension training on the sparkling coastal strip of the south east. Now, with their own little boy, they have moved to the urban sprawl of Sao Paulo to care for the children of their colleagues.

There is in Brazilian Portuguese no word for 'settle down'.

10. *Patience Repaid*

Indian Subcontinent 1930 to 1991

News travels slowly, if at all, to Potinga. Letters and papers have to come to Curitiba, then down the fast road with the thundering soya lorries to the port of Paranagua, but then along the winding, unmade coastal road to the remote community of Potinga, where a wooden sign points to the agricultural project of CEBADER. Frequently, the letters do not make it. Frequently the telephone fails to work for hours or even frustrating days at a time. But when, early in May 1991, David Stockley strode out of the dusky evening already swarming with mosquitos and into the rough little bungalow in the clearing in the rainforest, he knew that there had been news.

Joyce was a calm, sensible woman, trained in a London teaching hospital and schooled by nearly forty years as a missionary in the poorest parts of the world. She was standing at the cooker, bringing untreated milk to the boil three times for their coffee. She kept her back to her husband as she told him what she had heard of the cyclone and the tidal wave that had hit Bangladesh a day or so previously. She heard the scrape of the chair as the big farmer lowered himself at the kitchen table, put his head in his hands and remembered.

*

Until the last few years when, foregoing retirement, David and Joyce had felt compelled to meet the need for a agricultural missionary in Brazil, all their lives had been given to Bangladesh. Like many BMS staff, David was the missionary child of missionary parents. He had been born in China. But it was to East Pakistan, as it then was, that the society had sent the young man who had rather floored them when he offered his services after leaving agricultural college. Doctors, nurses, teachers, yes . . . but they had no experience of using a full-time agriculturist. They had decided to send David to a country in its infancy, born in August 1947 out of the bitter and bloody process of partition. India for the Hindus. Pakistan – West, and, a thousand miles across India, East – for the Muslims.

David had found himself in one of the poorest countries on earth. Although East Pakistan was less than one fifth of the area of West Pakistan, it was home to over half the total population. Millions of people tried to scratch a living from its low-lying soil, often deluged by monsoons or battered by the winds that roared up from the Bay of Bengal.

The tiny Baptist churches, never strong, were in disarray; partition had cut the Bengal Baptist Union in two and severed the struggling Christian communities now in East Pakistan from the sources of higher education and theological training around Calcutta. After the inter-faith bloodletting that had accompanied partition, Pakistan was a consciously Islamic state. To be Muslim was to be patriotic. To be Christian in East Pakistan was to be in a minority of three to every thousand in the population. Most of those Christians were poorly-educated converts from Hinduism. It was hardly surprising that they sought quiet survival rather than the proclamation of the Gospel to their Muslim neighbours.

Although East Pakistan remained primarily agricultural, independence had brought the beginnings of industrialisation. Chittagong was being developed as the chief port of East Pakistan. At Chandraghona, the hospital that had once set Dr Teichmann's heart plummeting, was blossoming. The Karnaphuli paper mill, one of the largest and most successful of the country's industrial projects, provided electricity for the hospital in 1953 and an operating theatre in 1955. The coming of electricity made X-rays possible, indeed vital as the demands on the hospital soared with the establishment of a hydro-electric scheme on the Karnaphuli. The little 'leper colony' that had begun with two lonely people on a hill was now, with government support, the country's premier centre for leprosy research and treatment. When Dr Bottoms left in 1960, he was to be replaced by Dr M. W. Flowers, but by 1965 the hospital would be ready to appoint its first Pakistani Medical Superintendent, Dr S. Choudhury.

Later, David Stockley's work would be entwined with the hospital at Chandraghona. But in 1954 it was to the district of Khulna, where the BMS was working with small churches in thirteen villages that the Stockleys went. The town of Khulna itself was changing fast, with jute mills, paper mills and a shipyard dependent on the port of Chalna. It was easy for the people of the town, newly prosperous, to forget that in the surrounding countryside nothing had changed for generations.

Then, gradually, there were changes. The people became aware of a new farm. Nobody seemed to mind them looking curiously or even shyly entering it. Strange crops appeared on the edge of the farm nearest to the road. There were crops grown in other areas of East Pakistan but rarely seen in Khulna – different varieties of rice and of bananas, sweet potato, groundnuts. There were crops never seen in Pakistan at all, and a Western visitor would have been startled to recognize lettuce and French beans.

The people watched. The crops thrived, as David knew they would, for he had tried them out away from the road before transferring them to his 'shop window'. When he

judged that the people were ready, David had gone to them
on their little bits of land, with his packets of seed and his
patient explanation. This variety of rice grew faster and
needed less irrigation than the type they were using. Their
children would be healthier if they ate green vegetables as
well as rice. The 'Khulna Uplift Centre', David's model
farm aimed at improving agricultural methods and the
living conditions of the people, was not only strong on
agricultural know-how. It was also strong on psychology
and imagination.

Imagination and enthusiasm are catching. During 1960 a
bemused Assistant Secretary of the BMS in London had
found himself inundated with day-old chicks, packets of
vegetable seeds and gardening tools. David Stockley, never
one to hesitate when things needed doing, had appealed to
children in British Sunday Schools for equipment for
Pakistani farms. There were now other agricultural
missionaries working for the BMS – John Smith in Diptipur
in Orissa, Alan Casebow in Yalemba in Congo, Ian
Pitkethly in Angola. There was a limit to how many day-
old chicks could be handled by a secretary in Gloucester
Place. Now David Stockley was making noises about goats!

In a conference centre in Derbyshire, a group of Baptist
men came to the rescue. In 1961 the Baptist Men's
Movement set up 'Operation Agri', to help meet the needs
of agricultural mission. By 1964, when David came home
on furlough, Operation Agri was well into its stride.
Calmly he handed over a shopping list of things he needed
to take back to Pakistan. Two large irrigation pumps; some
60-egg observation incubators; a large semi-automatic
incubator for a thousand eggs. Oh, yes, and a boat.

Sitting at the kitchen table in Potinga, David remembered
exhausting but happy years. Very short on personal
comfort for him, his wife and their children. Very short on
material recompense, yet, as David explained repeatedly,

'The gleam in the eyes of someone discovering he can do something himself to overcome his problems – that is our reward.'

After eleven years at Khulna had come Chandraghona, where the patients needed good food then and farming skills when they went home. The hillside behind the hospital, cleared of jungle, produced pineapples and papaya. Local farmers watched experiments with irrigation, strains of rice, breeds of cattle and poultry, even fish, and, emboldened by David's readiness to brave the bank manager on the subject of loans, formed co-operatives. David found himself in demand as a consultant as his ideas were tried out in other areas of East Pakistan. His 'catalytic' work aroused the interest of Oxfam. Then, in November 1979, had come the natural storm that precipitated the political one.

The news that had come along the dirt road of the litoral of Parana in 1991, news of a cyclone in which perhaps 200,000 people had died, brought it all back. The cyclone and tidal bore in November 1970 had killed half a million. David had surveyed the area by helicopter, walked extensively over ravaged acres of land, and then covered the kitchen table of his home with soil-testing kits. His children helped as he mixed chemicals with samples of soil.

'The question,' he explained, 'is what can grow now. Tons of soil have been moved. Fertilisers and soil salts have been leached to different areas. Look, that's starting to change colour . . . We have total destruction of all the farming of the population round here. Still, perhaps that means,' he pondered, watching the test tubes, 'that we have a clean sheet on which to work.'

The clean sheet enabled David to persuade local farmer to try a new 'miracle rice'. Researched in a Philippine institute but never before tried in Bangladesh, it treble the rice crop. It was perhaps proof of David's favourite assertion that 'disaster equals opportunity'.

If the natural storm was heartbreaking, the political one was terrifying. There was in East Pakistan a legacy of resentment against West Pakistan. While the East of the nation produced the money, the West spent it. The Pakistan government's refusal to recognize the election majority of Sheikh Mujib added to the bitterness at its inability to deal with the disaster of the cyclone from a thousand miles away. The rebel army of Sheikh Mujib began its struggle for autonomy for East Pakistan. The advice on the World Service was for expatriats to leave the country. In Rangunia, the local farmers, planting again after the cyclone, begged the Stockleys to stay. They stayed, identifying themselves with the people they had come to serve as so many missionaries had done before them through bloodshed in Jamaica, in China, in Congo. All that David would write home was that 'Two months of the country's history should be eradicated as terrible things have been committed by both sides of the country. Tremendous loss of life and property; so much so that the cyclone and tidal bore become something insignificant.' Even so, as thousands of people fled to India and India itself came into the conflict with Pakistan that issued finally in the creation of the republic of Bangladesh, crops were harvested round Rangunia and people saved from starvation.

The story of BMS involvement in Bangladesh was not over, though doors were soon to begin closing. For a while it was obvious what help the Society could give to the new country and to the Bangladesh Baptist Sangha. It could give £40,000 from a Baptist relief fund to help refugees returning from India rebuild their lives. It could offer support for the surviving Baptist membership of under 10,000 in a hundred-odd churches in the Sangha. Lack of leadership in the churches remained a problem, although there had been a Baptist Pastors' Training School and a College of Christian

Theology in Dacca since the mid 60s. It would help with the updating of the hospital at Chandraghona.

Then in 1975 Sheikh Mujib was assassinated and the republic replaced by the first of a series of military regimes that raised the Islamic consciousness of the nation and became increasingly unwelcoming to overseas missionaries. By 1990 there were just five BMS missionaries, all women, in Bangladesh and the life of Bangladeshi Christians was perhaps more difficult than ever.

In Potinga, Joyce carried the coffee to the table and placed a hand on her husband's shoulder. It had been a long and often sad story.

*

In the late 1940s, the Principal of the Woodstock School, sponsored by a group of missions in the Himalayan mountains of India, sought permission to make an ornithological survey with a difference.

Dr Bob Fleming regularly studied birds in the Indian mountains. Now he dared to ask for permission to extend his treks and his studies into the mountains of Nepal, the closed kingdom of 54,000 square miles between the subcontinent of India and Tibet.

He hardly dared to hope that the permission he sought would be granted. Nepal was medieval in its way of life, with every aspect of its culture and the lives of its ten million people grounded in Hinduism. Dr Fleming had seen an old postage stamp of Nepal, depicting its mountains, rivers and plains, and sitting as ruler over them all, the Hindu deity, Shiva.

Yet, amazingly, the reply to his request had been 'Yes'. And 'Yes' again in subsequent years, so that this time he dared to take with him on his bird-watching trips, medical colleagues who found much to occupy them in the remote mountain villages far from the fertile Kathmandu valley.

At the end of each trip, packing away the dispensary equipment as well as the binoculars, the friends left sadly. They knew that many missionary societies were working as close to the borders of Nepal as they dared. They knew that, although it was forbidden by law for any Nepali to change his religion, there were Nepalis who had heard the Gospel while visiting India and had returned to keep alive their new faith in secret. Dr Fleming longed to share with the Himalayan villagers good news about Jesus Christ; for the sake of the people themselves, he dared not do so. Neither did he dare to hope for dramatic political change in a country unchanged for centuries.

*

The advice from the 'church growth' consultant of the United Christian Missionary Society, newly in co-operation with the Baptists in Orissa in 1956, was similarly lacking in hope. It was a counsel, if not of despair, than at any rate of pragmatism. The growth in the churches of the Kond Hills before the war had been mainly amongst the people of the Panos tribes rather than amongst the Konds themselves. While Dr Donald McGavran understood the patient longing of the Baptist missionaries to see the Konds themselves come to Christ, they must see the importance of putting resources where they were likely to meet with most response. If, he suggested at the end of a flying visit, they really wanted to make one last attempt, they should send a team of the best all-Kond Christians, together with a missionary, into the most favourable area of the hills.

'Give it six months,' he conceded. 'Then if a few scattered baptisms are all that occur, you must face the fact that the Konds are no more responsive now than they have been for the past fifty years and you must concentrate on the Panos.'

His hearers looked at the sky and reminded him that this was June. This was the start of the rainy season which would last until October. The one last effort up into the hills and through the forest to take the Gospel to the Konds would have to wait for the better travelling conditions of the cold season.

*

As the 1956 rains fell, apparently holding up evangelism in the remote hills of Orissa, elsewhere in India the priority for discussion was organization rather than evangelism. The readiness for independence, for which the BMS had looked for so long, was now in evidence in the Indian churches, but it stirred mixed emotions in the hearts of the missionaries.

There was no closing their eyes to the fact that the newly-felt urge for independence was born of political pressure and nationalistic fervour as much as theological conviction. Since partition, there had been a growing emphasis on India as a Hindu society in which people of other faiths were regarded with the politeness and constraint to be offered to 'guests'.

Political independence had brought in its wake a reaction against the legacies of the Raj, a rejection of British imports, a re-evaluation of Western ideas. For the churches it was urgently necessary to be seen to be free from the trammels of western influence. For the 140 BMS missionaries in India, it was necessary to rethink their rôle, to relinquish adminstrative responsibilities, to recognize that they were now to be partners with, rather than leaders within the national churches. Even the vocabulary of mission was changing as words like 'mission station' and 'mission field' became out of place in the new concept of 'partnership'.

If the process of handing over of power was hard for missionaries, forced into a sudden change of status, it was hard also for the churches. The Council of Baptist Churches in North India established in 1957 brought together Baptist groups with a diversity of experience and strength. Into the Council came the Bengal Baptist Union, which had reluctantly been forced to reform without the churches in East Pakistan, and the Uktal Christian Church Central Council, already working in co-operation with the American Disciples of Christ through the United Christian Missionary Society.

Into the Council, too, came the Churches of the Mizo District, strong, well on their way to 50,000 members, eager to accept responsibility for their own affairs, and the Baptist Union of North India, still facing the unresolved question of 'success' and 'failure' that had tormented Isabel Angus thirty years previously. Many thousands of men and women in North India owed their education, their health, some even their lives, to the patient work of missionaries in schools and hospitals. That fact had not made them any more receptive to the Christian faith that the missionaries had sought to share.

Nor, in the sparkling island of Sri Lanka at the other end of the subcontinent, had the years of work by Baptist missionaries in schools made any real inroads into the Buddhist community. After independence for Ceylon in 1948, the number of overseas missionaries allowed by the government was strictly controlled by quota and BMS support for the Sri Lanka Baptist Sangamaya, established in 1958 with a membership of less than 2,000, became largely financial. The vocabulary and the structures of mission had changed within one decade; the task for the churches in most areas of India remained no less daunting than before.

*

The little group of Kond men, clad in loin cloths, long hair knotted high over their heads, walked barefoot along the stony tracks over the hills. They were making for Pokari in the hill tracts twenty-five miles south of Baliguda. Seven years earlier a small Baptist church had been formed in Pokari when a group of Konds had asked for teaching from Panos Christians. For five years the little church had survived uneventfully. Then, during the rainy season of 1956, the church at Pokari had burst into vibrant life. Twelve miles to the east, in the church in a village called Terovadi, the same process had taken place at the same time. The Holy Spirit had waited for the coming neither of the cold season nor of the team of evangelists proposed as one last effort by a church-growth consultant. Once the movement amongst the Konds began, there was no stopping it. Both Pokari and Terovadi stood on important foot-tracks used by traders. It would have been impossible, even if they had wanted to, to keep the news of what was happening in the churches to themselves.

As the group of Kond men descended the rocky mountain slope, they could see first the small paddy fields and then the thatched huts of Pokari. They moved quickly, for it was important for the people of their village to receive the help they needed. As many as forty families were anxious to learn about the God whom the Christians worshipped and of whom they had heard other Konds speaking in the market places. With encouragement, the families were ready to give up the sacrifices they offered to placate the evil spirits of the forest, spirits that destroyed their crops and made their children ill. But they knew they first needed to learn more.

For the visitors, it was a journey full of significance. For the pastor at Pokari, coming out to greet them and to listen, it was the tenth such request for help in two years. Soon, Christians from Pokari would be on their way back with the messengers, to talk and teach, to prepare individuals, couples, whole families for baptism, to assist with the building of a mud and wattle church. In that year of 1958, there were 400 baptisms in the Kond hills. The following year would see over 700 and the year after that over 1,000. Between 1956 and 1961, fifty new churches were formed in the Kond Hills.

The new Christians worshipped with all the joy and intensity of those released from a fear which had over-shadowed every area of their lives. Organized into groups of churches within 'walking distance' – which could be twelve miles of jungle-clad hills – of each other, they were eager to learn more of their new-found faith. When pastors' wives or missionaries offered village women a class in literacy, village health and Bible study, the women put their babies on their hips, walked for eight miles, studied for three hours and walked home to prepare dinner. When a church was asked to act as host for a three-day course for teenaged girls, the men of the church took four valuable days from work in the fields to dig cooking trenches and prepare cauldrons of rice and curry.

In the 1920s the desperate need of the people of the Kond Hills had been for medical care. Now Udayagiri had its hospital, the Moorshead Memorial Hospital opened in 1939, renowned throughout Orissa for the skill of surgeon Stanley Thomas. Yet medical mission was not without its tensions. Balancing the necessity of raising finances for the hospital, through the treatment of private patients, against the urgent needs of the poor members of the Kond community was proving, and would continue to prove, a delicate juggling act.

But now the race was on to bring literacy to people who had to memorise the Lord's Prayer and the Kui hymns that they accompanied with their cymbals and drums. New schools were opened at Gudipori and Mallikapori, the largest Christian village in the Kond Hills. In 1963 boys studying at the High School in Udayagiri were offered a

Christian home in the new Millman Hostel. In the churches of Berhampur and Cuttack, Christians who had themselves been students of Oliver Millman in the Cuttack High School took the opportunity in the funding of the hostel to repay something of what had been given to them.

With both children and adults learning to read, it was time for a new Kui version of the New Testament. The old version had been overtaken by advances in the study of the language, and the Bible Society was ready to finance a new translation. Overseen by Baptist missionary Bruce Henry, four Kui Christians began primary translation work. Their rôle was to translate into Kui from the Oriya version of the New Testament, a draft which had later to be checked against the Greek. It was an arduous task but one which brought flashes of enlightenment and pleasure to the western translator. For Kui, the language of folklore and tribal songs, could offer its own fresh vitality to the human stories and dialogue of the gospels. Here at least, in the Kond Hills, was 'partnership' as, at its best, it could be. Not imposed by structures but born of reciprocal giving between missionaries and some of the least sophisticated people in India.

*

1962. In East Pakistan the chicks organized by Operation Agri were arriving at Khulna. In North India, Baptist missionary Leslie Wenger was heading a Baptist delegation grappling with preliminary moves towards an ecumenical union of Protestant churches there. In the Kond Hills, sixty new churches had been formed in the past five years. Perhaps most amazingly of all, in Nepal, Margaret Robinson, the first Baptist missionary to be sent to Nepal, joined the staff of the Shanta Bhawan mission hospital in Kathmandu.

The political change for which Dr Bob Fleming had not dared to hope had come in 1951. Revolution had ended the traditional regime of the Ranas. With Indian help, the deposed king Tribuvan was restored to the throne. Breaking the conditions of his restoration, he was to prove an absolute monarch. He was also in no doubt about the changes he wanted for his country.

For a country with less than 500 kilometres of roads, one airport, six megawatts of electricity and no university, he planned developments for which he knew he would need advisers and technicians from India, China, Japan, the United States, Europe and the United Nations. Such guests were to be invited to share in the task of service and 'nation building'. The one price the king was not prepared to pay for the bridges and dams and universities and government administration he needed was the dismantling of Hindu society.

The basic medical care offered by Dr Fleming and his colleagues on their visits to the remote mountain areas had not gone unremarked and had not been forgotten. Just a few years previously, they had had to plead to cross the border into Nepal. Now they found themselves invited back and asked to provide medical care in Kathmandu and Tansen.

They themselves were representatives of Methodist and Presbyterian mission boards, yet they had seen that the opportunities offered to them should be available to any interested societies and churches. In March 1954, at Nagpur in central India, the United Mission to Nepal (UMN) had been formed as a project of the National Christian Council of India. It brought together eight missionary societies committed to working together as one organization. Its first venture was to set up clinics for women and children in the Kathmandu valley. These initial plans were swept away in the flood of patients that overwhelmed the clinics and necessitated the adaptation of the Shanta Bhawan palace into a hospital as quickly as possible. The name, appropriately, meant 'dwelling of peace'.

In Kathmandu in 1962, Margaret Robinson, sent by the BMS to work with the UMN, although the Society was not yet a member of the mission, found herself in the dilemma which would continue to face missionaries in Nepal. On duty, she was in no doubt how much her skills and her care were needed in the wards and maternity unit of the hospital. Yet she could not talk to her patients about the Christian faith that motivated her work.

Still at least, off duty, she was able to put the frustrations and longings she felt on the wards into words and to discuss and pray about them with colleagues from the hospital or the mission's girls' high school in the city. Margaret knew that many workers with the UMN were working in ones and twos in far lonelier situations than hers. For them, there would be no shared faith, no prayer meeting. They had to keep their Christian faith alive alone, without the fellowship and corporate worship considered so important in churches in England.

Nepali law still forbad anyone to change his religion or to encourage other people to change theirs. On one occasion an elderly woman had argued doggedly and successfully in court that she had been converted simply by reading the New Testament for herself and that no other human being had been involved. Margaret knew, however, that in the town of Tansen, where the Mission had a hospital, eight Nepalis converted to Christianity had served eleven months in prison and the pastor who baptized them had received a sentence of six years.

By 1962, the eight societies initially involved in the UMN had swelled to twenty-one. Workers supported by Christians in Japan, the USA, Australia and Europe worked together with pooled resources. In 1966 the BMS sent a second missionary, Sylvia Slade, to work in the Tansen hospital and two years later they sent their first teacher, Margaret Kingsley. In 1968 the BMS became a member body of the UMN. From then on Baptist missionaries took to Nepal a wide range of expertise from dentistry and physiotherapy to engineering and rural development. They shared in the challenge of 'nation building' and at the same time patiently sought to show by example the Christian faith they were not permitted to preach. A decade after entering the United Mission, the BMS had become the third largest contributor of personnel. Within another decade, Nepal was to be the Society's third largest sphere of partnership in mission.

In February 1991, Baptist missionary David Payne flew in to Kathmandu en route to Butwal near the southern border of Nepal. After research in industry and at university in Britain, he was returning to Nepal to help manage a Materials Technology Department, providing an information, testing and development resource for urban and rural needs in Nepal.

Around him David could see the evidence of forty years of rapid development of the country, by no means all of it positive. Like Carey, like Isabel Angus, like generations of missionaries, he tried to capture for friends at home the reality around him. Like them, this missionary at the close of the twentieth century used the language of the concerns of his day:

More buildings, electricity, telephones, cars and 'high technology' are some of the more obvious signs in the urban areas; the disparity between rich and poor, the neglected rural areas, urban pollution and the silently approaching environmental disaster of deforestation are the more sobering aspects.

David had returned also to a country seething with political ferment. A 'popular movement' for which some had given their lives had been pressing for democratic reform. People were calling for constitutional rather than absolute monarchy, for multi-party politics. Within a few weeks there were to be elections which could change the political face of Nepal again.

The changing of the religious face of Nepal was taking place more quietly. Nepal remains a Hindu society but one in which some freedoms are now granted to those of other faiths. The Christians who for decades have had to gather in small groups for Bible study and prayer are now allowed to erect buildings for worship, although they are still not permitted to evangelize.

The missionaries of the United Mission to Nepal have been able to be involved in the life of the Protestant church of Nepal only in a personal and limited way, never in an official rôle. Yet, encouraged by their example and perhaps fortified by the awareness that the missionaries themselves know what it is to have to keep alive a lonely faith, that church has grown from a handful of believers in the 1950s to perhaps 25,000 forty years later.

*

The formation of the Church of North India (CNI) on 29th November 1970 was a celebration shot through with colour and shimmering with light. By day – for the events took two days – the congregation of 3,000 was accommodated not in Lucknow Cathedral itself but in a huge marquee in its grounds. Into the marquee, with its red and gold awning, the colours of the badge of the new church, wound the procession of new bishops in white robes and red stoles. At night, as songs from different areas of North India rose into the cool air and dancers moved expressively through the clauses of the Lord's Prayer, lights shimmered on the edge of the marquee and a large illuminated map picked out in the darkness the various dioceses of the CNI.

There was much to celebrate. The Church of North India was bringing together the Anglicans, the Congregationalists and Presbyterians of the United Church of North India, the Methodist Church in India, the Council of Baptist Churches, the Church of the Brethren and the Church of Christ. Ernest Madge, representing the BMS, watched almost in disbelief as an Anglican bishop received Communion at the hands of a Methodist woman. It was an achievement that bridged cultures as well as denominations. Within the area of the CNI, spanning all of India except the four southern states, Christians spoke nine regional languages and six major tribal languages

Yet, if there was much to celebrate, much remained unresolved. Leslie Wenger, after fifteen years of negotiation on issues of ministry and communion, knew that the most thorny question of all, the rebaptism of believers who had been baptized as infants, had yet to be faced in practice. And, although the Council of Baptist Churches was being born into the CNI, many Indian Baptists were not at the birthday party.

Of the member bodies of the Council of Baptist Churches, only one, the Uktal Christian Church Central Council, had voted unanimously to join the CNI. Jugal Mohanty was to be the first Baptist bishop of Cuttack, caring for one of the largest diocese in the new church. But in other areas individual Baptist churches had made their own decisions to join or stay out of the new body. Some areas, including Mizoram, were today conspicuous by their absence. The BMS had promised to remain in partnership with Baptist churches both within and outside the CNI. It was to be a partnership not without the pain of misunderstanding and the hurt feelings of resentment.

So much changing; so much unresolved. With the laying

on of hands, it was impossible for the Baptists present to forget another legacy: the little community by the Hooghly, the passion of Carey, the quiet strength of Hannah Marshman; the clatter of the printing press, the walls of the college rising by the river. Four of the new bishops of the CNI – Reuel Soren, an Anglican, Dharmadas Pradhan, a Presbyterian, Dinesh Gorai, a Methodist and the Baptist Jugal Mohanty – were graduates of Serampore College. Nothing could undermine that legacy or undo that work. Yet today the college was once more beset with problems and there were few Baptists on the staff. There were in fact fewer and fewer British missionaries in India. The English Baptists had arrived in India in 1793 as illegal immigrants in the eyes of the state. They were now in 1970, in the eyes of the state if not of the people, increasingly unwelcome guests. When Leslie Wenger had first taken his place at the negotiations for the CNI fifteen years previously, there had been 140 BMS missionaries in India. Now, as the Indian government made it more and more difficult for new or returning missionaries to obtain visas, there were no more than thirty. By 1990 there would be just four, all of them women.

The dancers on the stage moved through the phrases of the Lord's Prayer. 'Thy kingdom come; thy will be done.' Baptist Christians in the two areas of India where the churches had become strongest and most alive were seeking the kingdom and the will of God in different ways. The churches of the Kond Hills, unsophisticated, miles from Delhi, beset often by militant Hindu opposition, yet had their 'bishop' and their place in the CNI. The churches of Mizoram had made the alternative decision and in 1970 were putting their energies instead into their own infant concern – the Zoram Baptist Mission.

The Mizo Christians had their own legacy from the BMS. It was a passion for mission amongst their neighbouring tribes and in other areas of India. By 1990 the Mizo Church of over 40,000 members would have 150 missionaries in various areas of India. At the start of the century, Dr Teichmann on his medical visit into the Lushai Hills had heard the Mizo Christians singing on the hilltops. By the close of the century, the Mizo Choir would have sung in churches and cathedrals all over the world.

'Thy kingdom come; they will be done.' The badge of the Church of North India incorporates a gold cross and chalice set against a red background. Behind the cross is a white lotus flower, dear to the heart of every Indian. For the lotus is the symbol of the spiritual quest of India.

11. Not Strangers but Friends

Towards 2000

'And so the baby Jesus was born in a strange town because Mary and Joseph were forced to make a journey. A few days later they were all in great danger and had to move on again and flee to Egypt.'

The first Christmas of their exile, the Angolan Christians were telling in the villages of the Lower Congo their nativity. It was a story from which as refugees themselves they drew comfort and strength. It helped to put behind them the nightmare journey through the forest between Angola and Congo, guided through the minefields by the freedom-fighters of the FNLA. It helped to put into a context they could understand the pain of seeing their children taken from all that was familiar to them and so weakened by hunger that they could not stand.

The Angolans were resilient and hardworking people; they were used to oppression by the Portuguese colonial regime. The Christians, identified as they arrived by 'seeker groups' and linked with each other so that the Kibentele church exploded from 500 to 13,500 in a few weeks, had in wordly terms lost everything. They had lost homes, possessions, livelihood. They had not lost their faith. More, here they were, as they unfolded their Christmas narrative and revitalized the Congolese church, ready to pass it on.

There were other factors to help the Angolans who crossed the border in the early 1960s, a stream in '61 and '62, a flood in '63 and '64, half a million in four years. Unlike some of the world's refugee people, they did not arrive as unwelcome strangers in a totally foreign land. They came in a sense to their own – the people of the Lower Congo were of the same tribe as the Angolans and both spoke Kikongo, though with a different dialect – and their own received them. Their Congolese brothers and sisters offered them land for huts and planting in the small villages. Space was not at a premium. The drift to Kinshasa had seen to that.

They came, too, to Christian missionaries who had shared their suffering in Angola and who, by 1962, were reassembling to share their exile in Congo. David Grenfell, Angola Field Secretary, was there writing letters all round the world, seeking aid. Margaret, his wife; Jim and Pep Grenfell; medical staff Rodger Sheilds and Betty Gill; teachers Phyl Gilbert and Vera Harrison; as the Angolans arrived, the missionaries too were arriving.

Nurses Edna Staple and Jean Comber were based before long at Kimpese; for the rest of the missionaries in a house in Kibentele life was communal and cramped. Dr Sheilds slept surrounded by his medicines. Jim Grenfell had a little room of corrugated iron sheets attached to the verandah. Access to the bathroom was via a wardrobe in somebody's bedroom. The proximity forced upon them afforded ample opportunity for discussion and, as the immediate short-term need for food for the refugees gave way to long-term strategy, for planning.

The United Nations High Commission for Refugees had divided responsibility for relief work in Lower Congo into three areas, one under the Roman Catholics, one under the Congolese Red Cross and one – the area round Kimpese where the Baptist work was focused – under the Protestants.

As the international spotlight fell on the Angolan refugees and much-needed aid began to arrive, David Grenfell was presented with the kind of logistical challenge in which his spirit delighted. Rice arrived from the United States, sugar from Poland, dried milk from Holland. Food supplies arrived by train with no warning, so that there was a mad scramble to unload tons of food and protect it from sun and insects. Then a cement company offered its siding, its warehouse and wages for a team of refugees to unload the food. In 1964, 26,000 food rations were distributed in one week.

What had started as a response to a crisis of uncertain duration became a way of life. The people who had emerged from the forest to be received at Kibentele and given food rations, a machete, a hoe and seeds – a million and a half vegetable seeds from the Church World Service of America made the difference between starvation and survival for thousands of people in 1965 – began to harvest their land. Babies were born in the little dispensary at Kibentele, which later had a new maternity ward, and their elder brothers sat side by side with Congolese children in the string of new primary schools.

The Landrover fitted out by Rodger Sheilds and Betty Gill as a mobile dispensary became a familiar and welcome sight as it crossed and recrossed an area of 4000 square miles, on the move for six years. With the doctor and nurse went an Angolan evangelist who had been hospital chaplain at San Salvador.

Although all the Angolans were ready to plant, harvest and before long produce a surplus of food for trade with Kinshasa, not all were peasant farmers. Many were craftsmen. But they were tailors without sewing machines, carpenters without lathes, tinsmiths with no tools. Two hundred sewing machines provided by the Baptist World Alliance and bales of khaki cloth brought the Angolan tailors back to life. Masonry tools gave the builders, too, a new job to do, replacing the hastily-erected huts of the early days with more permanent structures. In 1968 a grant from the UN High Commission for Refugees made it possible to build forty more primary schools.

So much to do; so much goodwill; increasing resources. From an apparent tragedy had come opportunity. Certainly the children from the primary schools who passed the examination for one of the coveted forty places in the one secondary school at Sona Bata had an opportunity they would never have had in Angola. The school had once been run by American Baptists. When they withdrew from it, Canadian Baptists took it over, and one of the first young men through its doors was Alvaro Rodrigues, who would one day become General Secretary of the Angolan Church. Others of the 300 to 400 youngsters who studied there would go on to Kimpese and beyond.

And yet . . . And yet . . . There were inevitable tensions, dilemmas, always a need for sensitivity. Angola missionaries were working on 'the patch' of Congo missionaries and this could so easily appear 'a field within a field'. A field moreover that received resources that others also needed and could not have. A field visited by television crews and MPs and Senators and directors of relief agencies.

It was vital, too, to steer clear of political controversy. The Angolan freedom-fighters were divided, quick to accuse missionaries of partiality to either FNLA or the MPLA.

And as exile seemed to be becoming a way of life, over it all hung the question: how long should the aid operation be allowed to continue? How long before it bred resentment in the Congolese who had welcomed the refugees so generously?

But in the schools and in the theological colleges the seeds were already being planted that would one day make it possible for the Angolans to go home – and for the Angolan church in particular not just to return but to survive and grow. Forty Angolans trained in the Lower Congo for the Baptist ministry. Like all young ministers, they had much to give to the Congolese church in terms of spiritual vitality and enthusiasm and much to gain in terms of experience. They gave and received in the Congolese churches. One became pastor of the largest church in Kinshasa. Although they perhaps did not realize it at the time, they were in effect getting ready to go home.

*

Home. In 1975 the Angolans were going home. A coup in Portugal in 1974 seemed at last to have opened the way for independence for Angola. It was not only peasant farmers and craftsmen who were ready to return. Those with apparently most to lose – teachers in secure and stimulating posts, the pastor of Kinshasa's largest church – were eager to rebuild their country. They longed, too, to be reunited with fellow-countrymen who had never crossed the frontier but spent fourteen long years in hiding in the forest.

It was a homecoming full of hope and excitement but marked also by the awareness of what had been lost. Of 200 former Baptist church buildings only two were still standing. The mission buildings at Bembe and Kibokolo were in ruins. The San Salvador church buildings, focus for worship for many Angolan Christians, bore the evidence of use as a dancehall and bar. The lives of those who had eked out a living in the forest were scarred, too, with the less tangible but equally real wounds of privation and fear.

Yet the determination to rebuild was as strong as ever. For the Christians, encouraged by Jim Grenfell, that meant reforming church life. The experience and training they had gained in exile spurred them to re-establish church fellowships, pastoral care and worship. In 1977, just two years after their return, they were ready to found the Evangelical Baptist Church of Angola.

The homecoming and the hope were to be short-lived. The newly independent country became, as was so often the case in that era, a battleground for external powers and politics. The MPLA government, backed by Cuba, was challenged by UNITA forces armed by South Africa. Once again Angolans – 90,000 of them – fled across the border. The relief work in what was now known as Zaire had to begin again.

But with a difference. This time the Zairians were rather less welcoming. They had missed the Angolans when they left. The withdrawal of half a million hardworking people who had produced food and other goods for Kinshasa as well as for themselves had been a shock to the Zairians. There had been famine in 1975 and 1976 and in the destabilising of the economy lay the seeds of greater economic problems in Zaire in later years. It was hardly surprising if the Zairians did not welcome back with open arms those whom they felt had in 1975 left them in the lurch. This was to prove in any case a smaller and briefer relief operation than the earlier one with the refugees confined to a more limited area.

Some of the Angolan pastors remained in their own country, continuing evangelism and pastoral care for those who stayed. For those who moved with the refugees, life was different this time. In the 1960s they had easily found a rôle in the Baptist Churches of the Lower Congo. In 1972, the three Baptist 'communities' of the Lower, Middle and Upper River had come together in the *Communauté Baptiste du Fleuve Zaire* (CBFZ – Baptist Community of the River Zaire). It was far more difficult for the Angolan pastors to fit into the unwieldy structures of a national body. They had skills and energy and ideas that were not being used. So they began to write – to produce for Christians a series of booklets on some of the thorny issues of the time. Christian marriage, the upbringing of children, traditional African medicine.

The partnership of the BMS and the people of Angola

was and would continue to be a partnership of shared suffering, seized opportunities, tenacious hope. The Angolan people never lost the spiritual vitality that had sustained the refugees, spilled over to their hosts and warmed the hearts of the missionaries. By the time that a peace accord between Angola, Cuba and South Africa finally held out in 1988 a real promise of political stability, the Baptist Church of Angola had doubled its membership from 10,000 in 1959 to 20,000 in 1987. The BMS had shared in a partnership of persistent and rewarded faithfulness and in a story that had captured the imagination and tugged at the hearts of many people, especially young people, in England.

*

In the BMS Summer Schools of the 1960s, young people swam, played cricket on the beach, swarmed on to coaches, washed up after dinner, crept along the rambling corridors of large old country houses and schools for midnight feasts, and wandered after dark into the grounds hand in hand with people who, in several cases, would one day be their husband or wife.

They also read the Bible, individually and together, sang missionary hymns as yet untouched by the wave of hymn-writing that would break on the churches in the 70s, and listened to missionaries home on furlough unfolding their experiences. In the mid 60s hundreds of teenagers from Baptist churches caught something of the suffering of the Angolans and the excitement of the Konds, and for some of those young people life, and what they intended to do with it, would never be the same again. From one summer school in 1966 emerged two future missionaries and two future ministers.

The vision of 'Africa for Christ' which had come to

Tom Comber and George Grenfell in the Young Men's Missionary Societies of the 1870s was as compelling as ever. But it came now to a generation more highly educated, with more specific skills and with a different perception of its relationship with what would come to be know as 'the third world'.

The BMS itself became ready over two decades to welcome young men and women who were not necessarily saying 'I feel called to be a missionary in Africa for the rest of my life', but who explained instead 'I have trained as a pharmacist or a physiotherapist or an engineer and I would like to offer at any rate three or four years of my life in Christian service overseas'. Indeed offers of short-term service from people trained in particular specialities seemed in the 1970s just what was needed in the partnership of the BMS with the new-born *Communauté Baptiste du Fleuve Zaire*. For that was a partnership in which the initiative in requesting the help of people with particular abilities – 'we need secondary school teachers for Ngungu and Kisangani, a theological tutor for Kimpese, a nurse at Pimu' – lay with the Zairians.

It was perhaps little short of miraculous that the Baptist Christians spread along the great scything length of the Congo river had in 1972 come together in the CBFZ. There was much that would naturally have kept the Baptists of the Lower, Middle and Upper River in their three distinct groupings. Vast geographical distances brought daunting problems in communication. The deep-seated roots of regionalism and tribalism added to the practical difficulties of language – not only of up to 350 different tribal dialects but of the fact that the population of Bas Zaire, formerly Lower Congo, spoke Kikongo while the common language in the middle and upper regions was Lingala.

Against these divisive factors worked other considerations making unity for Zairian Baptists desirable. They had not only a common origin in the work of the BMS but an ongoing common need for practical help from the Society – personnel, transport, grants, scholarships. While there were leaders in the churches who feared that any reorganization would threaten their personal status and power, there were many other educated young lay people who recognized that the body of Christ should be, and be seen to be, one.

These considerations were faced in the real world not only of theology and spirituality but of politics and legislation. The politics of the authoritarian regime of President Mobutu added significant pressure for the formation of the CBFZ. In contrast with the hierarchical structure of the Roman Catholic Church, Mobutu found the plethora of Protestant churches and groupings, often with breakaway sects and schisms and sometimes embroiled in scandals, unnerving and exasperating to deal with. Legislation was introduced to force the Protestant groups into one umbrella organization, and the Congo Protestant Council, a purely consultative body, was replaced by the *Eglise du Christ du Zaire* (ECZ) – the Church of Christ in Zaire). All Protestant churches, or communities as they were to be called, had to belong to the ECZ. The presence of foreign missions was hardly in accord with the move to make national life as 'authentic', as Zairian as possible. The BMS, needing to hand over its property to Zairian Baptists was faced with the question – did it hand it to one body or to three? If to three, how could it divide the valuable resources of the Secretariat in Kinshasa, in Bas-Zaire?

That the answer finally was that the BMS should hand its resources in Zaire to one and not three Baptist bodies was the result of many hours of dialogue between representatives of the Society, of the ECZ and of the three Baptist communities. For the BMS the process demanded great patience. For the Zairians, the same process, through discussion to consensus and submission to the will of the group, was a normal way of proceeding.

The thorny issue of a General Secretary for the CBFZ – none of the three former communities was likely to accept the leader of either of the others – was resolved by recalling from study in Belgium Pastor Mfwilwakanda, formerly education co-ordinator for the Protestant Council. Pastor Mfwilwakanda served for five years before being succeeded by Pastor Koli. For the Zairians the appointment of Pastor Mfwilwakanda had the virtue of having been reached by compromise.

Such a culture was a far cry from the individualistic priorities of western society. Some of the new missionaries eager to use their skills in the service of the CBFZ succeeded in crossing the culture gap. They came to understand the Zairian way of making decisions and the restraints of working with an autonomous church. Others found it harder to do so. For them frustration and bewilderment simply added to other problems. It was never easy to translate expertise gained in British universities and laboratories and hospitals into often lonely situations with inadequate resources in Zaire.

'Why,' a missionary might ask – especially when tired by climate or illness, exasperated by the non-arrival of mail or of an elusive part for vital transport, disappointed to uncover a new Christian in some act of dishonesty – 'why am I here and not there? Who decided I should work here teaching midwifery when I have more experience and interest in orthopaedic nursing than in obstetrics? I know I would be more use in a different area.' Or 'Why, with all my education and experience, do I have no more say in the running of the local church than any Zairian church member? I can see what is going wrong there.'

Across the culture gap, officers of the CBFZ, struggling to keep pace with a Zairian Baptist church growing from

40,000 members in 1960 to 200,000 thirty years later, limited by a national economy plunging ever nearer to chaos and creating great hardship and temptation for many people, balancing the needs of three still distinctive regions, plus Kinshasa, might ask: 'What is wrong with this missionary? Why can't she see that we have to take into account not only her particular skills but the fact that it was the turn of this area to have a new nurse? Why can't she accept what we as a group believe to be best for everyone?' And 'We remember the missionaries who were our fathers and mothers in God and who served us all their lives. Why don't these new missionaries stay?'

Against such a background, in which hopes on both sides slipped into frustration and disappointment, many missionaries were able to serve the Zairian church and people with expertise and love. They staffed the Bible Schools at Bolobo and Yakusu. They worked in agricultural projects at Kimpese, Ngombe Lutete and Ntondo. They provided medical consultants at Kimpese and directors for the hospitals at Pimu and Yakusu. They coped with an authoritarian political regime intent on stamping a Zairian identity on the nation and threatening at times to take control of Christian hospitals. In 1990 there were seventy-eight BMS missionaries working with the CBFZ. Yet it had become impossible to ignore the rate of turnover amongst them. It was impossible, too, to ignore the feelings of many missionaries that, now that there was no Field Secretary and pastoral care of missionaries was the responsibility of the CBFZ, they did not always receive the pastoral support they needed.

Once again, as in 1972, the way forward had to be to sit down and talk. A Consultation in Bas-Zaire in the summer of 1990 proceeded through worship and teaching towards unravelling some of the difficulties and disappointments of the partnership between the BMS and the Zairian church.

How did each one see the role of the missionary? Would it be possible for the CBFZ to be assisted in its pastoral responsibilities towards them by a pastor who was himself a missionary? How, in a nation with a collapsing economy, might the CBFZ move towards greater financial self-sufficiency?

As the plain talking on both sides was continuing, so was missionary life. Much further up the river, a little plane circled above what was – hopefully – Pimu and its new hospital. For the Ellett family of Kinshasa it was an adventure they would describe in a prayer letter to friends in England.

'Has anyone been to Pimu before?' asked the pilot. 'Can anybody see a river?' The whole family looked down from the six-seater Missionary Aviation Fellowship (MAF) 'plane. We were 700 feet above the green ocean of jungle. We looked and prayed . . .

Travel in Zaire is not easy, not certain, but it was worth the journey to get to Pimu. Our turn had come to play our part in the Pimu project. While Bob repaired the electricity supply system, Ruth and the girls helped the hospital staff in the pharmacy and prepared for the new intake of student nurses. They packed bandages, counted pills, cleaned shelves and catalogued textbooks. It was a privilege to be part of a hospital team providing health care for an area the size of Wales . . .

One of the joys of being in Pimu was the way in which the local church and mission supported each other, and the closeness and bond of fellowship which existed between the people involved. At Pimu we could see and experience the life of a Zairian village. The well maintained thatched mud brick houses. The warmth and friendliness of the people.

There was adequate food while we were there but the children had the swollen bellies of malnourishment. Most of the population is heavily infested with intestinal parasites. Adrian Hopkins the missionary doctor at Pimu explained that this led to anaemia . . . The combination of this and any other illness can easily be fatal. It was noticeable that there were lots of small children, fewer teenagers, less adults and very few people over sixty. People die very easily here . . .

So much that was warm and encouraging; so much that was fragile. Human lives hanging, as they had hung despite a century of medical mission, by a thread. Relationships between BMS and CBFZ strained, though never broken. Over it all, the threats of a teetering Zairian economy and a discredited political regime. Nothing was certain in Zaire.

On the night of 22nd September 1991, one of President Mobutu's para-commando brigades, angry at the non-payment of a promised pay rise, went on the rampage at the international airport twenty kilometres from Kinshasa. By morning, the airport buildings were a shell, and other soldiers with grenades and bazookas began storming and looting stores in the capital. All the years of resentment at political corruption, economic chaos, hardship and hunger exploded amongst soldiers and civilians alike and the rioting spread from Kinshasa to Kisangani and on to other Zairian towns.

Fuel supplies were destroyed; copper and diamond mines were attacked; ransacked buildings were set on fire and the country's infrastructure collapsed. Some Zairians died; others, already hungry, saw prices for what food there was available soar.

In Kinshasha, the BMS missionaries who had known that it was probably only a matter of time before civil unrest shook Zaire, gathered in one home. The advice from the

British government and from Zairian friends concerned for their safety was that they should leave. On the Thursday, after prayer and Bible reading with Pastor Koli of the CBFZ, the Kinshasa missionaries were evacuated from the airport now ringed with French and Belgian troops sent in to protect their nationals.

Upriver, missionaries from Kisangani and Yakusu were airlifted, some by the Missionary Aviation Fellowship, to Bangui in the Central African Republic and then to Brazzaville in the Congo Republic. Missionaries from Bolobo also left via Brazzaville. Within days, of the seventy-eight BMS personnel who had been working in Zaire, only five remained, in the relatively quiet area round Kimpese. By December 1991, only one, pharmacist Gwen Hunter working at IME (L'Institut Medical Evangélique), Kimpese, was left.

On retreat in North Wales the missionary families relived and shared their experiences and prayed together for Zaire. They began to unravel their feelings of shock, disappointment, guilt at having to leave the Zairian people facing unemployment, hunger, lack of medicines, and of bereavement at separation from Zairian friends.

It was impossible and, though fact-finding visits began almost at once, would remain for some time impossible, to conjecture what lay ahead for the nation, for its churches, and for the partnership of BMS and CBFZ. The hopes and plans of the Consultation just one year earlier were suspended. The relationship was not.

*

Dawn in the city of Bangkok. The Buddhist monks in their saffron robes were out early with their wooden bowls, soon filled with food by almsgivers. The English woman who had come to Thailand to start a new life was also awake early. It was hard to sleep when her mind was full of the tantalizingly difficult Thai language and its script. Jacqui had embarked on Thai, knowing that, like Chinese, it was a monosyllabic tonal language. Merely a difference in tone – rising, falling – could change the sense of a word and make for hilarious or embarrassing mistakes.

Nothing, however, could really prepare a westerner for a script made up of forty-four consonants and forty-eight vowel and dipthong possibilities, read from right to left with no space between words and no punctuation marks. Patient though her language teachers were – and Suntari in particular was becoming a friend, seeming sometimes as eager to learn as to teach – this was certainly a language to keep a new student awake at night.

Nothing, in fact, could prepare a westerner for life in the city of Bangkok. Beautiful in many ways; the tiered roofs of the Buddhist temples glowed with golden spires; before long the 'floating market' would be busy on one of the canals that crisscrossed the city. But Bangkok was also snarled up by its chaotic traffic, choked with fumes, its crumbling pavements baked with relentless heat. It was not an easy city in which to start a new life, a new language and to study a new culture and religion. Eleven years in Bangladesh had taught Jacqui Wells much about Bengali, about Islam, about how to get close to the Bangladeshi women and children. Now, in 1987, denied a visa to continue work in Bangladesh, she had come as the first missionary of the BMS to work alongside American, Australian and Swedish missionaries of the Thailand Baptist Missionary Fellowship within the tiny Church of Christ in Thailand. . .

As the monks walked quietly back to their temples and Jacqui pored over her sheaves of notes, in another, sleazier street of Bangkok a young woman was also making a bid for a new life as she leapt from the window of the brothel into which she had been sold by her uncle. It took all the courage that is born of desperation, but she had heard that, if she could reach the Women's Emergency Home run by Christians in the city, she would be sheltered there.

Hundreds of thousands of girls, some little more than children, worked as prostitutes in Bangkok. Some had drifted to the city in search of work and money because the traditional ways of life – rice and sugar growing, fish and duck farming – were harder and harder to sustain for the poor and uneducated. Other girls had been snatched from the remoter areas of the country or sold by their families to supply the spin-off areas of tourism, now Thailand's third largest money-maker. Few of the girls were fortunate enough to escape or to have any chance of a different way of life.

But for this girl there was now that chance. Just a few months earlier, women of the Church of Christ in Thailand, appalled by a fire in a brothel on the island of Phuket, in which several girls had died, one because she was chained to a pole, had opened the New Life Centre in the city of Chiang Mai in Northern Thailand. The girl who had leapt from the brothel window was one of the first girls to study there. For her and for other young women from the hill tribes, the chance to learn literacy and handcraft skills gave them the means of earning a living other than with their bodies.

By 1990, Jacqui Wells was also living not far from Chiang Mai – and learning yet another language. She had come to Thailand to work amongst the women of the Karen, one of the hilltribes of the north-west. So it was Karen and its Burmese characters that now came into her mind when she closed her eyes at night. But it was also Karen that filled her days. 'I shall learn the Karen language from the people,' she insisted. 'If you can get alongside people and work with them, you pick up the language because you want to communicate.' This was the language study not of the classroom but of the home, the fields, the Bible study group, of shared work and shared laughter.

Jacqui was certainly the kind of woman who got alongside others. In Bangkok she had been close to her language teacher, Suntari. Now, to her joy, Suntari had become a Christian, the first Christian in her Buddhist family. Not an easy decision to make for the wife of a government official but one that in the end had to be made, because she saw in the lives of Christians a contentment that she lacked in her own.

Perhaps that event spoke more than any other of the kind of partnership that was evolving in Thailand. Not the dramatic partnership through headline-making thick and thin of the BMS and the Angolans; not the large-scale, structured partnership of BMS and CBFZ. It was the partnership of one or two individuals – Jacqui had been followed to Thailand by Chris and Geoff Bland to work with the small churches of the Udan Thani in the poorest, driest area of the country, the north-east – with Thai people.

That partnership involved having the grace to learn a very difficult language and an oriental culture. It involved building, as Jacqui was to build at Chiang Mai, not a western-style home but a typically Thai house near the Centre for the Uplift of the Hill Tribes.

The victims of Thailand's rapid movement from an almost totally agricultural way of life towards western-style materialism were the young people of the hill tribes. The Centre was for them. Here for them was an educational programme and the help they needed with new agricultural skills that would make it possible to resist the lure of Bangkok. Here, too, was Christian training to strengthen the Baptist churches: Bible study with Jacqui for the Karen women; training for pastors and lay leaders.

Nothing can stop the rapid social change of Thailand but

what can perhaps be done is to stop the closing off of the options for the poor. A new life for Jacqui Wells, a new partnership for the BMS, involved the opportunity to put before at least some young Thai men and women the possibilities of a new life for them too.

*

El Salvador. Like the name of the Angolan city, where the Baptist church for a while became a place for soldiers to drink and meet women, the name of the smallest country in Central America similarly bears witness to 'The Saviour'. The Salvadorean people carve little wooden crosses and paint them in the vibrant primary colours, red, blue, yellow, that speak of life and hope. Yet a girl of thirteen who has never known anything but civil war sees 'My People' like this:

> My nation is a nation at war; it is a nation where
> hunger is never absent, where folk live pursuing hope
> and die without ever achieving it.
> My nation is a nation where armed struggle has become
> part of life, where the death of millions is nothing.
> My nation is a nation where 'war' is between brothers,
> where God does not exist for the rich, and for the poor
> He is all that is left where tyrants govern.
> My nation is a nation which despite suffering rises up
> every morning and sets out on its way to God,
> and sets out on its way to its daily tasks,
> where the rich live in palaces surrounded by riches,
> where the poor live on the street surrounded by misery.

El Salvador. In a small town in the east of the country, it is market day. As the sun rises high in the sky, the cattle and pigs drink gratefully. A long queue of people has also formed at the tap in the market place.

A few streets away a small boy is sick and his parents seek out Baptist missionary David Quinney-Mee. Although David is a pastor, not a doctor, he gives what medicine he can.

'But why,' he wants to know, 'is the child sick again? You came just a few weeks ago.'

'It's the water,' the mother explains. 'He gets sick because we have to drink dirty water.'

'But surely – ' the queue at the tap now stretches round the pens of the animals – 'you have clean water.'

'Oh, no, pastor, only on Thursday mornings. That's really for the animals. The rest of the time we have to buy our water. Clean water costs more than dirty water. We can only afford dirty water, so our children get sick.'

Perhaps it would be possible to ask the town's mayor if the water turned on once a week for the pigs and cows could be turned on on other days for the people? Perhaps if the people offered to dig the trenches and lay the pipes themselves?

Two or three people, then five or six, announce that they are willing to approach the mayor. Yet they are aware that, as soon as they organize themselves into a group to do so, they will be regarded with suspicion by the authorities, branded as subversive.

But the Salvadoreans, especially the women, are courageous people. They have grown used to oppression, first by the colonizing Spanish, then for nearly two centuries by a small ruling faction within their own nation. They approach the mayor, who explains that he has to discuss the matter with the military. The officers will need the names and identity numbers of all the people asking for clean water for their children. Each visit to the town hall, where the mayor is flanked by soldiers, makes the people, especially their spokesmen, more vulnerable, more easily picked out by the military. At the end of the dangerous road which the people have dared to walk and which they cannot retrace comes the answer to their request. No water.

David Mee offered himself to the BMS in the late 1980s specifically for work in El Salvador. As a Baptist minister working in England, he had in fact first approached the Baptist Union, hoping that it might be possible for him to be seconded to work as a minister with the Baptist Association of El Salvador. Such an approach was significant. It indicated the extended horizons of the Baptist Unions of Britain, Wales and Scotland, traditionally concerned with mission at home, and their increasing involvement with the worldwide Church. In another significant move, pointing to the ever closer relationship of Unions and Missionary Society, the BU had referred David to the BMS. Like James and Susan Grote, who were to follow him to El Salvador in 1991, David had been profoundly moved by the assassination of Archbishop Oscar Romero. The Archbishop had championed the rights of the people (over half the population had no adequate housing, a quarter of a million children received no education) against the handful of families who for generations had become rich and powerful on the fruits of the coffee crop produced by the poor. For that championing of the rights of the poor, Romero had been assassinated while he was celebrating Mass.

David Mee went to El Salvador in 1988. He went to a country in which 70,000 lives had been taken in nine years of civil war. Hundreds of thousands of refugees, from the population of five million, had fled into Honduras or were dispersed within their own country. He went as a pastor with a brief from the BMS to bring the wholeness of the Christian Gospel to the community. He began to explore his brief amongst a community of displaced men, women and children in Sensuntepeque in the east of El Salvador. By spring of the following year, the BMS had entered into an agreement for full mission partnership with the Baptist Association of El Salvador.

Many members of that Association were living with the awareness that in El Salvador whose who aligned themselves with the poor in the struggle for justice – even church workers trying simply to establish basic education or feeding programmes for the children of their neighbourhood – were perceived as a threat to the government and the military. For the question in the sunlit Thursday morning market place and in the darkened atmosphere of the mayor's office, armed guards at the door, was not simply about water and health. It was about power.

Soon after David Mee arrived in the country, death squads intensified their efforts to pick off the leaders of church, civil rights and trade union groups. Carlos Sanchez, General Secretary of the Baptist Association, received death threats. A young woman member of Emmanuel Baptist Church, working with women's groups, was abducted, tortured and murdered.

In 1991 David and Rachel Quinney-Mee and James and Susan Grote work with the Baptist Association as pastors and preachers and also as supporters, enablers, friends of the people. It is a partnership of mutual solidarity. They themselves learn from those they watch beside, from their patience and their hope, for 'My nation is a nation which despite suffering rises up every morning and sets out on its way to God.'

*

Suffering and renewal. Opportunity and frustration. Patient befriending. Watchful solidarity. It was into such a richness of relationships that the BMS moved during the second half of the twentieth century. There were many changes in mission style. Some were born of a new understanding of the resources of the world church. Some were achieved through persistence and hard work. Some were thrust upon the Society by political upheaval. Yet there was more to come.

In the closing years of the 1980s and into the 1990s, dramatic changes swept the world stage: the fall of the Berlin Wall; the end of Communist control in many Eastern European countries; the disintegration of the USSR following 'perestroika'; the moves toward closer union within the twelve nation states of the European Community. These, in a breathtakingly short time, formed the stuff of which history is made. They formed too the backcloth against which, 200 years on from Carey, Fuller, Ryland, and Sutcliffe, the BMS was to celebrate its Bicentenary.

Since its birth in the widow's house in Kettering, the BMS had had several homes, most of them in London. The move to Baptist House in Didcot meant not only a new home but the speeding up of the growing relationship with the Baptist Unions of Great Britain, Wales and Scotland.

In a world of changing frontiers, crowded air-routes and political refugees, old distinctions between those Christians traditionally concerned with mission at home and those committed for 200 years to mission overseas no longer hold good. When the opportunity arose to work with the small Baptist churches of Belgium and Italy, the Society was ready to provide personnel, the Unions to provide literature. When, in events unthinkable a decade earlier, the chance came in November 1991 for British Baptist leaders to visit the Union of Evangelical Christians/Baptists in the USSR, four General Secretaries of the Baptist Unions of England, Wales and Scotland and of the BMS went together. They visited the great cities of Moscow, St Petersburg and Kiev, to see how links might be formed with Russian or Soviet or Commonwealth churches – not for the first time in Russian history, the names and language were being overtaken by events.

'What have we to tell? What have we to give?' Those, for two centuries have been the questions on the lips of British Baptists concerned with mission. In many cases they were the immediate response, a well-intentioned response, to the tumbling of political systems at the end of the 1980s. 'How can we help the churches of Eastern Europe?' Slowly British churches are recognizing that the questions are also 'What have we to learn? What may we receive from Christians who have lived out their faith through generations of political oppression?'

Beyond Europe, a Conference in Korea of the BMS and its mission partners in Asia, Africa and South America emphasized the need for fully shared decision-making. In a world of cross-cultural possibilities, the Society's role is sometimes to be not instigator but enabler, helping to finance a Brazilian missionary couple working in English in Guyana, Mizo missionaries to work beyond India, Bangladeshi pastors to be trained in the Philippines.

If the British churches have the grace to make a Macedonian call themselves, who might come over and help them?

In the summer of 1988 the Young People's President of the El Salvador Baptist Association came to Britain for the Baptist World Youth Conference in Glasgow. With that visit came the opportunity to study and to visit British churches. Maria Josefa Hemandez, or Josefita, came into the churches with the stories she had to tell, of her own life, of her compelling faith, of her suffering and resilient people. The stories were unforgettable; she herself went straight to the hearts of the British Christians.

When Josefita went to visit the Baptists of the Cambridgeshire village of Histon, she lived in the village for three weeks. She spoke to children in their schools, parish councillors in the village hall, community leaders and the constituency MP, opening his eyes in a way no one else had been able to do to the political injustice in El Salvador.

With the stories came the underlying message of the mutuality, the need both to teach and to learn, give and receive that, two hundred years on from Carey, lies at the heart of mission partnership.

'If someone comes to us from Britain,' Josefita said, 'they can teach us from all the Bible knowledge they have. Whereas we can teach you how to live together and love each other. We can both learn.'

What British Christians received above all from Josefita they have received also from Indians, Brazilians, Zairians who have travelled on scholarships or fellowship visits: an unforgettable picture of what it means at the close of the twentieth century and the brink of the twenty-first to be a disciple of Jesus Christ.

Index

This index contains a selected list of people, places and events.